The Journey Of A Dream

What Goes On Backstage Of The Arena Of "Achieving A Dream"

Gilbert James

Into Thine Hand
4141 NW 39th Ave
Fort Lauderdale, FL 33309
www.intothinehand.com

The Journey Of A Dream

Copyright © 2011 by Gilbert James

All rights reserved. No part of this book may be reproduced or transmitted in any form or by any means without written permission of the author.

ISBN: 978-0-9841231-1-7

All Scripture quotations are taken from the Holy Bible, King James Version, Copyright © 1977, 1984, Thomas Nelson Inc., Publishers.

Dedication

This book is dedicated to My One and Only Daughter, Gilline James. Though the journey of your dream be interrupted, as it is likely to be, may you stay on track. May you be persistent. May you ever be inventively strategic in outwitting your attractions and distractions, thus arrive at your intended destination. May All Your Dreams Come True And May You Be An Asset to God, Yourself and Humanity! May you never outgrow God, regardless of where the journey of your dream may take you, but involve Him in all of your plans and ever make Him your source.

Love,
Dad!

Table of Contents

Are You Ready For The Journey To Your Dream?	7
Meet your master contractor	12
Dream The Golden Dream	20
Let's Go Backstage	29
Construct Your Tomorrow Today	34
Plan To Sail Instead Of Fail	42
Approach Your Dream Professionally	51
Relate For Success	57
Invent As A Lifestyle	70
Train For Championship	76
Congratulations! You Have Struck Gold!	87
Preserve Your Mines, Enjoy The Gold	94
Take Five Steps To Harvest	101
Remove The Snakes From Your Grass	110
"Treasurize" Your Travel	121
Your Success Quotes	132

ONE MOMENT PLEASE!

Are You Ready For The Journey To Your Dream?

If you are looking for a "get-rich-quick-scheme," put this book down now and keep looking for other resources. If you have a dream and want to see it come true, keep reading. If your desire is to design and produce a dream, definitely read on!

While I was desperately searching for a way out of a stagnant lifestyle, I went into a businessman's office. There I saw a statement that caught my attention. It was written in large letters and was virtually unavoidable. This is what it said:" A sure way to miss success is to miss its opportunities."

I stared at that statement, for a minute or more, amazed at how true it was. There is no surer way to miss success than to miss its opportunities.

Success is mankind's number one profession. Like love,

What goes on backstage of the arena of achieving a dream

success is definitely a universal language. Every person in every nation under the sun, despite his language, color or creed, speaks the language of success. Every human being, regardless of whether he admits it or not, desires success - most likely the highest level Of success possible.

By reaching this far, it is clear that you either have a dream that you are longing to see come true, or would like to design and produce one. In the pages of this book, I am not promising you any miracle while you sleep. 'Dreams coming true' is what this book is all about.

To make your life not only a dream, but a dream come true, I declare to you that neither I, nor this book in and of itself, can accomplish that end. In all honesty, you are the center of attention in this arena. To be able to make this venture worth any more of your time, you must either possess a "super ambition" that is naturally you, or endeavor to acquire such ambition in its highest order. By this I mean to possess or acquire a desire to achieve or accomplish to such an extent that no thunder, lightening, hurricanes, snow, heat, creature or situation can stop you. The final destination for the journey of your ambition should only end at achieving and maintaining your intended cause.

The Journey of a dream is like the road that you travel daily. There are other commuters who are both duly traveling from their departure to their destination and have equal rights to that same terrain as you do. Some will arrive at their destination as intended and some will join the list of casualties.

What will make the difference for the list of successful arrivers? The answer lies in their adherence to the road rules. Some perceive the road rules as designed to assist with their successful arrival and some perceive them as restrictive and are only there to be violated or defied.

I presume that you have already figured out who is likely to successfully arrive. The ultimate factor in this saga is which group do you fit in, which will determine your successful arrival or otherwise.

Just like the road that you travel daily, your journey to your dream has road rules. They include stop lights and signs. There are times that the road rules will require you to slowdown, make turns, yield to pedestrians and your fellow commuters, climb hill-like turfs and go down slopes, cruise over ruff turfs and reduce your speed for safety.

Your journey will require frequent fuel refills and performance checks for assured continuation.

Your engagement in your particular venture as you journey to your respective dreams must be prefaced by your resolve to abide by the rules of your roads, to arrive successfully.

Are you willing to comply with the rules of the road from where you are to where you are going… from your departure to your destination? If your answer is no, then drop every desire or aspiration to start this journey and go back to being the means to making someone else's dream a reality.

However, if you are willing to adhere to the rules of the road or

What goes on backstage of the arena of achieving a dream journey to your dream or your destination, then step in absolutely and attack it absolutely. This is an absolute journey and is compatible with the absolute only. You pay the absolute price or don't even start and waste you precious time and resources.

CHAPTER 1
Meet your master contractor

Are you ready to build your empire? How far are you willing to go and how much are you willing to pay to achieve arrival? A shocking reality in the science of arrival is that whatever is your burning ambition, you won't arrive anytime soon winging it by yourself. You will, of necessity, need assistance from external resources. People should be at the top of this list, however, there is one other source that should be even above the top of your list. He should be placed over the entire course of the journey as well of the journey itself.

Pursuant to the human abilities which are riddled with inabilities, frustration, disappointments, discouragements, exhaustion, dead ends, believe it or not, you will need God every step of the way. He should be your master contractor. A striking reality that isn't always revealed immediately in ones life's travel is the fact that this journey is infested with obstruction, detours, distraction, glitters, aggravation and camp anything goes.

As you are seriously committed to reaching your full potential, in actuality, you are embarking on a journey to unravel many present ravels. You are embarking on a journey that will surpass the previously established status quos. You are embarking on a journey that will challenge the expected boundaries. You are now ready to take advantage of your opportunities though they may have always been there, and you may have never noticed or cared to use them. As a result, you will have become a standard setter and of necessity will attract Judases, Lot's wives, Lot himself, etc. The list is endless. Believe it or not, you are going to need God. You will need Him as your master builder.

You need 'this' master builder because He is the only one who can really stop you because He rules this, yes, His universe. If He stops you, you are really stopped, no one else can move you forward. If He enables you, no one else can stop you.

You are going to encounter times and situations where no one can help you, including yourself. In these times and situations you will need supernatural interventions and your best source, rather, your only source, is He.

The list of history makers, movers and shapers, finite human beings that He has raised up to destinations unknown, is endless and He is always willing to accept new candidates.

The very fact that you have ventured to achieve will make you different from those who have chosen a different path. This will

What goes on backstage of the arena of achieving a dream automatically attract vultures who will make it their occupation to destroy you, your aspirations and your achievements. With Him as your master builder, you really won't even need to think about them, He takes care of that.

You want to avoid resorting to Him as an afterthought, a spare tire or a last resort, when your back is against the wall. Believe it or not, He gives you the breath to accomplish. If He withholds His breath, you are declared dead.

Place this master builder in charge of building your castle so that it will be worth your investment beyond the bank, all the way into eternity. Psalms one hundred and twenty seven verses one through two says: "Except the LORD build the house, they labor in vain that build it: except the LORD keep the city, the watchman waketh but in vain. It is vain for you to rise up early, to sit up late, to eat the bread of sorrows: for so he giveth his beloved sleep."

Congratulations, you have acquired the universe's most able contractor to build your castle when you acquire the Lord. This fact is confirmed in the book of Psalms one hundred and thirteen verses five through nine: "Who is like unto the LORD our God, who is on high, Who humbleth himself to behold the things that are in heaven, and in the earth! He raiseth up the poor out of the dust, and lifteth the needy out of the dunghill; that he may set him with princes, even with the princes of his people. He maketh the barren woman to keep house, and to be a joyful mother of children. Praise ye the LORD."

Hello, the bucks stop with God! "The LORD killeth and maketh alive: he bringeth down to the grave, and bringeth up. The LORD maketh poor, and maketh rich: he bringeth low, and lifteth up. He raiseth up the poor out of the dust, and lifteth up the beggar from the dunghill, to set them among princes, and to make them inherit the throne of glory: for the pillars of the earth are the LORD'S, and he hath set the world upon them." This is recorded in first Samuel two verse six through eight.

With God as your master builder, your promotion is imminent. Psalms seventy five verses six through seven affirm that "promotion cometh neither from the east, nor from the west, nor from the south. But God is the judge: he putteth down one, and setteth up another."

Note that nothing was said about the north. The dwelling of the Lord is in the north as referenced in Psalms fort eight verse two: "Beautiful for situation, the joy of the whole earth, *is mount Zion, on the sides of the north, the city of the great King."* The connection between the Lord's city which is Mount Zion and His dwelling which is also Mount Zion is seen in Psalms fort eight verse two: "Remember thy congregation, which thou hast purchased of old; the rod of thine inheritance, which thou hast redeemed; *this mount Zion, wherein thou hast dwelt."* This truth is further affirmed in Isaiah eight verse eighteen: "Behold, I and the children whom the Lord hath given me are for signs and for wonders in Israel from *the Lord of hosts, which dwelleth in mount Zion."*

Sign your biggest contract yet. Submit your works to the Lord, your master contractor before production and it's a sure deal. In the book of Proverbs chapter sixteen verse three we are told to "Commit thy works unto the LORD, and thy thoughts shall be established."

Remove your contractor's portion first so there is no backlog and time will tell: "Honor the LORD with thy substance, and with the firstfruits of all thine increase: So shall thy barns be filled with plenty, and thy presses shall burst out with new wine." This is what the writer of Proverbs three verses nine through ten admonishes us to do. It is the writer's position that if you put God first in your distribution; God will put you first in His distribution. Who do you believe has the most to give and will give the most? A full barns and a prosperous harvest isn't a bad return for just putting God first in your relation to your resources and profit as is in reference here.

Since you acquired this contractor who is the Lord, trust his representation and follow his advice or you are using someone else's. Proverbs three verse five through six affirms this. It says "Trust in the LORD with all thine heart; and lean not unto thine own understanding. In all thy ways acknowledge him, and he shall direct thy paths."

Make the Lord your first consultation and consolation before any other commitment or subcontracting and that which you seek will come to you. This is affirmed in Matthew six verse thirty three which says "But seek ye first the kingdom of God, and his righteousness; and all these things shall be added unto you."

Remember that your daily guidance and motivation comes found your master builder who is the Lord, instead of any other source. We see this brought out in the book of Philippians four verse one where it says: "I can do all things through Christ which strengtheneth me." All means all and that's all that all means, as someone rightly said. So we can do all things needful, but it must go through Jesus Christ our Lord. This means that the apparent impossibilities are indeed possible if we go through Jesus Christ our Lord. So you know which road to travel both when things appear possible and when they appear impossible because it is 'all' things that should be done through Jesus Christ our Lord.

With this level of relationship with the Lord, your master builder, help is at your fingertip. We are reminded in Psalms one hundred and twenty one verses one through two where the psalmist says "I will lift up mine eyes unto the hills, from whence cometh my help. My help cometh from the LORD, which made heaven and earth." When you truly realize that it is from the Lord that your help comes, in whatever venture you undertake, then no venture will be too hard for you because nothing I too hard for Him who is helping you.

Do this and your success is imminent. Immediate success is immediate success but how long does it last is the million dollar question. Unscrupulous success is unscrupulous success which carries consequences and bears fruits of its kind. Good success is that which is justified, that which is earned. Most of all, it is that which is given or endorsed by God. The book of Joshua chapter one verse eight speaks of that type of success and how to get it. Observe: "This book of the law shall not depart out of thy mouth; but thou shalt meditate therein day and night, that thou mayest observe to do according to all that is written therein: for then thou shalt make thy way prosperous, and then thou shalt have good success."

Go all the way… total commitment in exchange for absolute accuracy. Sacrifice that which is not sure for that which is sure which is the will of God. The call is for the discipline to embrace that which is absolute, wholesome, sure and of the divine source. "I beseech you therefore, brethren, by the mercies of God, that ye present your bodies a living sacrifice, holy, acceptable unto God, which is your reasonable service. And be not conformed to this world: but be ye transformed by the renewing of your mind, that ye may prove what is that good, and acceptable, and perfect, will of God." This is what the writer of the book of Romans says in Romans chapter twelve verses one through two.

CHAPTER 2
Dream The Golden Dream

The Golden Dream

Dream that you will be a star.
Dream that you will win your war.
Dream you'll break your fencing bar.
Dream your payday isn't far.

Dream you'll see a brighter day.
Dream you'll meet a brand new way.
Dream of silver platter tray.
Dream they'll come without delay.

Dream you'll sit on a golden throne.
Dream you'll wear a golden crown.
Dream you'll know success unknown.
Dream they'll one day be your own.

The Journey of A Dream

The poem "The Golden Dream" was drafted to assist us with how to dream rather than what to dream. To dream that you will be a star means that you should strive to shine like a star in everything that you are planning to do or are doing.

You should strive to be numbered in the "A" category in your field. You should strive to be the best, or at least one of the best, in such a field. You should endeavor to ascend to all of its heights and descend to all of its depths.

That you will win your war means that you should view your struggle in life as a real war. In actuality, it is. The sooner you wise up and realize that there is real warfare out there being waged for your resources, especially your mind, the more ready you will be for the journey of your dream. As such, you must expect artilleries to be forthcoming, instead of only going forth.

For anyone, including you, to be labeled a winner, he/she must have been involved in a real competition, battle or warfare. Casualties must be counted as part of the cost of any warfare, both on the opposing side and on yours. To tackle this journey, you must resolve to win your war one way or the other. Success at any cost has it's price tag: to earn (own) it you must pay that price. It is only after it is paid in full that you rightfully own it.

That *you will break your fencing bar* means that as a person with an ongoing dream, what you are aspiring to become is always beyond what you are. Therefore, you are fenced into your present status, regardless of what it is, by will or by force. As a result, you should ever be striving to break the boundaries of your present status. And you must continue to break it until you reach your intended dream or dreams, as you move on to greater heights in life. Your life should never be lived for one moment without a dream or future target that you are aiming for.

That *your payday isn't far* means that even though others might be getting their pay today, it isn't necessarily payment worth having or of lasting value. Yours will certainly come someday and it could very well be today, if you stay persistent and faithful. However long it takes, and whatever time it comes, it will be worth the journey or wait. Regardless of how much resource is required of you, *you are willing to go the distance* and so the journey is never too far in your economy.

That *"you will see a brighter day"* means that regardless of how dark things may seem today, you should believe that they will be brighter tomorrow and expect them to be. They will be so because you are strategically working to bring them to fruition instead of a happen-by- chance approach.

You must realize that the cloud in the sky, dark or light, always moves. If you move in the direction of the cloud, you will always live under it. But if you move in the opposite direction, sooner or later the sun or the moon will be uncovered and you will see a brighter day.

That *you will meet a brand new way* means that you should always look for a more elevating way rather than a way that is struggle-free or easier. It may mean more responsibilities, but you must realize that with every higher position, comes new responsibilities. You must courageously accept that status when it comes because, as you travel with diligence, you will become the total sum of what you have been becoming.

That you are to *dream of silver platter trays* mean that you will be served, at some point of your journey, what you have been paying for with your own life and resources. And certainly, you rightfully deserve such. You should continue to feed on the thought that you will someday enjoy what you have been toiling so diligently for. You should dare to proudly claim it and so enjoy it when it comes. It is rightly yours! If you have earned or paid for something, it rightfully belongs to you who have paid its price. As such, it justly belongs to you. This product, status or person that you have proudly earned is your reward, not a gift. You have earned it.

That *they will come without delay* refers to a different concept than the twenty-four hour measurement. Whatever time your dreams take, you will be there to receive them. In your heart of hearts, you are seeing them come to reality soon, possibly very soon. Rather than sitting back, waiting for them to come, you have been working to make them come true as speedily as possible. Thus, they will most likely do just that.

That *you will sit on a golden throne* is the dream that one day, from your very own throne, you will reign. You will one day rule over a kingdom that you have worked diligently for. This will be a kingdom that you have built or paid for with your own substance. It will be one that is directly out of your own imagination, as the Lord enables you. It will be one that you have bought and paid for with your mind, sweat, frustration, isolation, patience and courage. Then it becomes golden in that it is of immeasurable value to you. You will have involved a lot, if not your all, in its construction. You must enjoy its privileges, endure its pains and gladly assume its responsibilities.

That *you will wear a golden crown* means that you will be crowned king of your very own kingdom. As such you will accept it with pride and dignity. You will wear it graciously because it is a symbol of your "accomplish-ability." Instead of a gift, it will be your reward. Gifts you receive freely, rewards you work hard and wisely for. Instead of a handout or an inheritance, it will be your wages, rightfully yours!

That *you will know success unknown* means you should believe that your dreams will go places. Believe that they will bring you success beyond your wildest imagination. Believe that they will climb the highest mountain, descend to the deepest valley, sail across ten thousand oceans and touch the whole world's hearts.

That *"they will one day be your own"* means that they all will be yours, someday!

Study the ants and do likewise. The average person goes through life without a long term plan regarding what he wants to get out of it or give to it. As such, he is consciously or unconsciously leaving himself open to hopscotch from one interest to the next, picking up on every passing fad. We hardly ever prepare a full day's plan, much more, plans for an entire life. There is a real possibility that you won't live to see tomorrow, although it is highly probable that you will. If God chooses to make you live, you will arrive unprepared if you didn't prepare for tomorrow's arrival. Imagine taking a trip to England and failing to prepare for the cold weather, food or your accommodations. If you hadn't planned or prepared for your arrival, you would arrive regretting the things you could have achieved or picked up on the way had you planned for it before. You could only reflect, in regret on things that are only available at your departing site and could only be acquired prior to your travel.

You may say that the Bible tells us not to take any thought for what we will eat or drink. It is evident from that passage and others that strongly urge planning for one's journey, that the issue under discussion is needs, instead of wants. In short, do not engage yourself in the process of "worrying" about tomorrow's needs. On the contrary, while you should not "worry" about your tomorrow, it is wise to plan for it and plan well. It is also evident that a properly channeled and working person rarely finds time to sit down and "worry" about how he/she is going to get food or clothes. He won't need to.

In the book of Proverbs the wise man Solomon advised the sluggard to study the ants and do likewise. They have no guide, overseer or ruler but they provide their meat in the summer and gather their food in the harvest. The Bible also clearly states in 2 Thessalonians 3:10, that "...even when we were with you, this we commanded you, that if any would not work, either should he eat.'" Sounds harsh? It's there.

What goes on backstage of the arena of achieving a dream

One of the most effective ways to find the formulas for greatness is to study the lives and legacies of great people. If you don't know where you are going for one moment or one day, more so, a lifetime, you are likely to end up nowhere.

Let's examine the lives and legacies of a few key people. Solomon, the wisest man that this world has ever seen, puts it this way: "Where there is no vision, the people will perish." [Proverbs 29:18] This includes you. On the contrary, where there is a vision the people will rise and live, including you. Can you figure out why he became so great that his greatness is still affecting us today? It is evident that his was a life of endless visions for both himself and his people. Solomon was a visionary.

Dr. Martin Luther King Jr., quite possibly the greatest civil rights leader the world has ever seen, puts it this way: "I have a dream..." Dr. King was quite clear about his dream and was proud to identify with it. He believed and personalized his dream. He both spoke and lived it. The whole world clearly heard what his dream was and the American people saw him live it right before their very eyes. It consumed his daily activities. He lived his dream.

Reality is a factor that every one of us has to reckon with throughout our lifetime. In reality, "the person, who is not using the working system or formula for success, is automatically using the one for failure."

The writer says "make 'YOUR' own dream or someone else's dream will swiftly make you." Use your God given resources to carry out "YOUR" dream strategically, yea, (the dream that God wants you to have) or you will be used to carry out someone else's dream.

As for Solomon, his life provides evidence of success in wisdom, wealth, "accomplish-ability" and their far-reaching effects. What Dr. Martin Luther King Jr. accomplished in his short life span of thirty-five years, most people haven't touched even in twice that time or more. Reality has taught many people, who have refused to face it head on and deal with it courageously, that it is a worthy factor to be reckoned with. On the other hand, many who have reckoned with reality have seen greatness, or at least a balanced lifestyle. As for me, time will tell. Success for me is not necessarily having wealth, popularity, fame or fortune, but step by step accomplishing my life's destiny or dream in the will of God.

CHAPTER 3
Let's Go Backstage

THE INVISIBLE PRICE

You may see him on the plain
Where he sits and rules and reigns.
He may have borne a lot of pain,
And have worn some deadly stains,
Might have tried and tried again,
Till at last they bought him gains.
So don't let your poor heart feign,
And contempt to cut his reign.
If you try and do not wane,
Then you too might well attain.

What goes on backstage of the arena of achieving a dream

The person who isn't using the working formula for success is using "the" working formula for failure. When you find the formula that works for your journey, preserve it, personalize it, utilize it, defend it and accept it as your strategy until it has served its time.

Success is relative to your "current" abilities, resources, perspective and aspirations. This journey is a lifetime venture. To the true visionary, success is as much a moment-by-moment, as a lifetime, venture. The moment that you stop winning, you "were" a winner.

"Customized" is exclusive. On this journey, there are many solo channels - you must be prepared to play your solo scenes when they arrive, because they will.

A dream is an attainable dream when you become its puppet! It's a consuming project… gifts you receive freely, rewards you work hard and wisely for. It requires all of you; all that you own and all that you didn't realize you owned.

The cost of this journey is all that you are and own. Success at any cost has its price tag; to own (earn it,) you must pay your dues (its price).

Let strategy be your policy and luck be a bonus. The pathway of this journey is a strategic one. The person who spends one moment of his life without a predetermined and working strategy is like the driver whose hand is off the steering wheel while his foot is pressing the gas pedal. The master contractor states in the book of Luke chapter fourteen verses twenty eight through thirty the following: "For which of you, intending to build a tower, sitteth not down first, and counteth the cost, whether he has sufficient to finish it? Lest haply, after he hath laid the foundation, and is not able to finish it, all that behold it begin to mock him, Saying, This man began to build, and was not able to finish." It is better to die on your way to a dream, than to live for one day without one.

The vocabulary of progress excludes the word "quit." Quitting is incompatible with progress. There is no place for "Lot's wives" (for looking back). It's against the gravity of progress to entertain or be entertained by the thought of retreating, even for a moment.

The journey of this dream involves taking the bull by the horns. If it becomes an obstacle in your way, you earn the right to tackle it. The "how" is the big question that you will need to answer. But if you can in any way travel another path, you may very well have conserved your valuable time, resources and your interpersonal pyramid.

"Practice makes professionals" and without practice any project will become absolutely impossible. For success to work with the highest level of positive results, you must make it the number one objective in every venture. It will work even better if you make it your way of life.

The hardest person to regulate is you. If you can successfully regulate yourself, you can more than likely successfully regulate others. Master the art of mastering yourself first, then you will have earned the right to master the art of mastering others.

Real success is the result of persistent processes of "starting

What goes on backstage of the arena of achieving a dream

over" and "starting better," instead of an overnight dream coming true while you sleep. The dream that is under discussion in this book is a dream that occurs while you are wide awake and as alert as you can possibly be, instead of while you are asleep. For this dream to come true, all your antennas must be up, your screws must be tightened and your eyes focused in one direction; your mission.

Stardom, celebrity status, championship belts, best seller classifications and other statutes of their caliber are preceded by multiple major project failure, years of concentrated practice behind the scenes, thousands of dollars invested or seemingly foolishly spent, the abandonment by ninety percent of family and friends, before the public finally accepts your refined, respectable evidence of real proven success. It is after you convince them by your unflinching commitment to your dream that they will accept you as qualified to present that dream to them.

CHAPTER 4

Construct Your Tomorrow Today

Your strings must be attached. A continuously successful person is a visionary. He is always professionally employed by, and diligently working towards, his future cause. He exists in the present but lives for the future. In the present he is a sojourner, in the future he is a citizen. The present is his desk or workstation but the future is his retiring habitat.

There is a special security and sturdiness about establishing a future cause, industry, empire or organization when you have assumed the role of working on it with your present (s). It puts your life into focus. It prevents you from being carried about by every wind of attraction that blows by. It prevents you from wasting valuable resources that you could have banked, stored or invested into enhancing or constructing your future empire. The earlier you can get this resolve down pat, the more of your lifetime you have left to contribute to the construction and operation of your future empire.

The Journey of A Dream

It is said that when Mohammed Ali was twelve years old, he not only knew what he wanted to be, he was already in training to be a boxer. Is it any wonder why he became the world's most acclaimed boxer, possibly of all times? Committing yourself to one industry, cause, vocation or organization for the rest of your life should be considered concentrating rather than restricting, enslaving or a loss of other options. It should be viewed as security, sturdiness, focus and the end of wasting resources you could have contributed to your dream or cause.

At that level, you are like the son of a king, heir to his throne. You are presently the owner of the inheritance, but you will possess it in the day that all the required factors are in place. If the king's son spent his effort and resources traveling towards other destinations, enhancing other projects than his crowning and was occupied with interests other than preparing for rulership, his future kingdom would be of no value to him because he would not know how to operate while on that throne. On the other hand, it would benefit him greatly if he channeled his resources toward his throne, gathering every resource necessary and perfecting the skills needed to be an effective ruler.

The process of time getting to that throne, if he plugs himself into it from now, would be a grand anticipation. If he started immediately to think, act and operate like a future king, it would be easier to operate as such when he assumes his real responsibility, when he sits on his throne.

Which organization is the right one for you? An organization, as the author sees it, is any venture that you or anyone formulates or undertakes that involves: 1.) an objective; 2.) order; 3.) work; 4.)

What goes on backstage of the arena of achieving a dream

people, including yourself and 5.) rewards. Has it occurred to you that people formulate and operate several (mini) organizations daily?

There are three major types of organizations as the author sees it that are critical to the mission of achieving your dream: 1.) physically required organizations; 2.) charitable organizations and 3.) vocational organizations. The first set of organizations is defined as the one that is required for life, for example, setting up and putting into effect your dietary structure, activating an exercise program, setting up and maintaining an accommodating environment, etc. The second is defined as "non-profit" organizations, those that are, to a greater extent, geared towards the needs of others formed to get money for the hungry, the sick, the mentally challenged, etc.

The third is defined as your vocational or professional organization, for example, your maid services, janitorial services, psychological services, physical services, human services, political services, automobile repairs, etc. One can start practicing to run his professional and charitable organizations effectively by being able to effectively run his physically required organizations effectively. In most cases, the level of management that one produces in his physically required organizations is quite likely the level he will produce with his professional or charitable organization.

You are virtually 'required' to both formulate and activate the first category of organization daily. The second and third, you choose to formulate and activate each day. The first you are expected to activate daily, but the second and the third are the ones that require all the professional motivation and perspective. They require the hard work, the brain bursting, the burning of midnight oil, taking the bulls by the horns, all the sacrifice, you name it.

The formulas of this book require a lifetime resolve and commitment to your particular vocation for you to be truly successful in it. By this, I mean that you are to choose a cause, field, organization or vocation that God wants you to be in, and vow to stick to it for life. You say, "But sir, you are advocating a lifetime commitment here." You got it right; I most certainly am! At this state you will have moved your destination from present to future. At this stage, you will have purchased your one-way ticket to your future empire.

You now will have plugged yourself into your home based industry or empire. At this stage, you will have become your true home based industrial agent. You are now fully qualified and officially authorized to professionally travel from your past to your present, from your present to your future.

Use your present do design your future and rewrite your past. You can change your past or future status by how you use your present. Take special note of the process of the transition previously mentioned, past to present, present to future. Your present is the intermediate connector to both your past and your future.

What you do in the present determines how people will view your past, and to the same degree it determines how they will view your future. The present is the period of time that we all have to work, to plan, to design, to achieve, etc. The future will meet you in the form of the present. Technically, there is no future because the future will always meet you in the form of the present. If we have to pass through the present to get to the future from our past, our present holds the key to determine in what light we shed on each direction.

Therefore, make maximum and productive use of your present(s). Regardless of what has and is predicted to happen to you or what your status was or is, your duty and only strategy as a perpetually successful person is never to worry about that, but to make maximum and effective use of your presents(s), to design your future kingdom and to rewrite your status of the past.

If you sit there and worry about either your past or your future, they will never change. Your best option is to master worry with positive action and make maximum and productive use of your present(s). Though you cannot change the events of the past, you can work towards changing your status and the views of others towards you with the effective use of your present(s).

Thus, the formula for being a good agent of your future empire is to make your present(s) your drafting board for its boundaries. And the formula for changing your past and future status is the same as above.

Be exclusively exclusive. Clamp yourself down to one specific field and be a master of it. You can never own all that the universe has in it. You can never know all that there is to know about everything. You can never give service to all there is to be serviced. Therefore, limit yourself to one specific field that God gave you the talent to service and master it.

Believe me, you will always find things that seem better than what you now have or ever will have. There are always better things to own. There is always external and apparently more influential knowledge to gain. There is always something that you "might" be able to give better service in. There is always an apparently more beautiful person than your spouse or spouse-to-be. However, when it comes to this portion of your mission, the test is how stable you can be, instead of how mobile you can prove yourself to be. What is important is how durable and reliable you really are, instead of how fluctuating you can prove yourself to be. One of the qualities that a perpetually successful person possesses is the virtue of stability instead of mobility, durability instead of fluctuation.

I used to teach a Sunday school class in a little ministry that was headed by a man whom I highly respected. He used to pick me up at my home on his way to the church. We would usually be with his wife, traveling each Sunday. One Sunday his wife was sick and he only had me to talk with while traveling. We began to talk about the planets, the stars, the sun, the moon, etc. We discussed the distance between us and them, how they gave light, what color they were in actuality, what they could do, what would happen if certain events took place and certain events did not take place. (He was the one doing most of the talking, I was mostly doing the listening.) He then switched to the human body, the numerous amounts of brain cells, the digestive system and many other wonders of the human make up. Then he went on to relate them to God and how He made all of those things, how He made them run on their own categorical laws and yet if He turned His back on them for one split second, all would go up in flames. It came out of my mouth (I am still puzzled as to how it ever came out) that I might need to get some information about the cosmos. He gladly turned to me and offered some books that he would bring for me to read. My heart almost jumped out of my body. I stammered and stuttered until I finally said maybe later. To date, I wonder if he realized the impact it had on me. I was already lost in the little amount of information he gave me,

What goes on backstage of the arena of achieving a dream let alone delving into the cosmos.

I realized then that it would be an impossible task to know everything there is to know or serve in all capacities there are to serve. Therefore I would need to clamp myself down to one specific field that God gave me the talent to learn about. To a person and his field, he is a master; compare him with the earth and he is a morsel, with the universe and he is a mite. Therefore commit yourself to one specific field and become a master of it.

CHAPTER 5
Plan To Sail Instead Of Fail

"*Design A Diagram*" written or memorized! Without it, you still need to start! Plan your foundation with big destinations. If you plan to build an elaborate future, be sure that you build an elaborate foundation. Spend the required, and in some cases, elaborate, amount of resources laying a solid and extensive foundation for your future empire and resist the pressure to launch it before it is time. Take lesson from the words of Jesus in Luke fourteen verses twenty eight through thirty. It says: *"For which of you, intending to build a tower, sitteth not down first, and counteth the cost, whether he have sufficient to finish it? Lest haply, after he hath laid the foundation, and is not able to finish it, all that behold it begin to mock him, 30. Saying, This man began to build, and was not able to finish."*

Similar to a physical building, the larger the intended structure, the more elaborate the foundation that is required. A good and sure foundation may take several years to build, but don't dare to cut it shorter than is required. Remember that just as a physical building is subject to good, bad and destructive weather so is your future empire, figuratively speaking. The strength, survival and success of your project depend as much on its foundation as it does on its structure and operation. Constructing or trying to construct a building on a flimsy foundation spells failure somewhere between bad and destructive weather. So, if you have to get your education, get it; if you have to establish your credibility, establish it; if you have to increase your popularity, increase it; if you have to do your research, do it; if you have to acquire finances, acquire them. Whatever foundational work you have to do, spend the appropriate amount of resources and time required to do it. Any other path would be a clear sabotage of your own valued project in the long run… you would be cheating on the most critical factor of its structure, its foundation.

Plan your construction without limitation. Planning for continuous success must be without a bung on its bounds. One of the critical mistakes people make in anything they have started or are planning to start is going into it thinking, "I am just going to test this out and see how it works." With this stiff jacket, they already doom themselves to mediocrity; they have created an option for giving up on some aspects, quite likely the seemingly difficult ones. They have set themselves up to ignore and leave them when they require just a little more effort and better planning.

For anyone to start anything and be continuously successful in it, he must plan for that venture to continue at least throughout his lifetime. The longer you plan for your organization to last, the more guarantees you have for its success. If that organization can be started and run as though it will continue for generations, it will have a sixty eight percent guarantee for success. So far, we have established the organization's destiny in relation to time. That is a very important aspect in your planning for continuous success.

There is another very vital aspect that should be included in your planning for the journey of your dream. This will determine your organization's destiny in relation to extent or expansion. This is the establishment of how large your organization will be; how far it will extend or how wide it will expand. Planning for continuous success in anything should contain long-term goals, in relation to time and also long-term goals in relation to space.

Your organization will more than likely remain within the bounds of expansion that you plan for it. From an optimistic perspective, it will potentially exhaust the extent of expansion that you plan for it. Even if your organization reaches a standing or running position, as long as room is left in your plans for it, it has places to go. However, if your plans for it are completed, your organization is limited until you make new plans.

The lowest extent of expansion that you should plan for is nationwide. But the best or most appropriate plan in this formula is for an international or global destination.

Join the dots of your plans. Preparation for continuous success should also contain directed and working sub-goals. The directed goals are those that are structured to carry you straight, without detour, to your major or long-term goals. For example, if your long-term goal is to be a leader, one of your directed goals should be that you should structure your life to live to understand people. Or if your long-term goal is to be a preacher, one of your directed goals should be to master the Scriptures. On the contrary, if your long- term goal is to be a leader, you would be off course if one of your directed goals was to learn how to cook. Or if your long-term goal is to be a preacher, you would be off course if one of your directed goals was to have as many concubines as possible. If your cause is lying directly west, you would be off course if you are traveling northwest.

The working aspect looks at the "workability" of the directed goals. If your directed goals fall short of working, you either have to find or design different ones or fail to reach your long-term goal or goals. For example, if you are climbing a hill and your steps are slipping, you are likely to fall at the critical point and you may never reach the top.

In terms of sub-goals, you must start climbing your mountains from their feet instead of their peaks. You must first be a student before you can become a teacher. Captains were first privates or constables before they became captains. The sub-goals may be subordinate but are still in context with your long-term goal or goals. For example, if your long-term goal is to be a captain, one of your sub-goals should be to become an officer or a constable first. Or if your long-term goal is to be a teacher, one of your sub-goals should definitely be, to be a student.

So, for you to master the journey of your dream, your planning must contain long-term goals as well as directed, working sub-goals.

Brand your plans. Remember to program and stamp or sign your plans with your seal of approval or signature before you send them out. Your plans must be designed so that they are uniquely yours. Whatever you send out there that comes out of your womb is your brand. It will speak volumes good or bad of you. If you have to go through the mill, so to speak, design and redesign, start over and start better, then that you must ensure so that once released, you are the proud owner instead of being afraid of identifying with your own production.

Your work should be a masterpiece within its own unique realm and if possible, compared to the world, if you please. Your plans must be so designed that the products of their production should be so crafted that even though they may sour through the premises of the world so to speak, their domicile should be you and you should be easily identified as their designer. Instead of assuming the posture of being afraid to identify with products of your plans, they must be so designed that you are proud to identify with them. They must be so unique that they solely fit you.

It may take a very long time for your own unique plans to take affect and receive accommodation in different realm besides yours. However, the further your rewards are from you, the more appreciative you will be when you get them.

It is important that you digest the following truth: If you allow other people, regardless of who they are to choose your rewards for you, you effectively become their slave. So, always be ahead in choosing your rewards, namely the ones that God wants you to have, and work hard and or wisely (strategically) for them.

Remember that you are within the bounds of a customized exclusive, even if they are out of context with the ones that the crowd is working for. The crowd or the majority can be the ones that need to be corrected or brought back on course. As a matter of fact, it has been found in that position in many instances.

For this formula, you are more than likely on course if you seek to part from the crowd in relation to your dreams. It can be more rewarding, and you can be more outstanding, in the process.

The more you practice this strategy and fill your life with it, the more you will find yourself becoming in control of your life. You will become a person who sets examples and standards instead of one who is a reactor, imitator or parakeet. This medal, your pending reward, you privately own until it is publicly given to you.

Never ever confuse rewards with gifts or dare to substitute them. They are as different as night is to day, or darkness to light. Rewards you work hard and or wisely for. Gifts, you receive freely. Rewards that are worth having are always accompanied by hard and or wise work. But in working, remember that if you use your head, you will save your strength.

Pass this test and your plans will fly. After ensuring that your plans meet God's requirements, the second most important criteria is this: always gear your plans to edify humanity or to meet the needs of your fellowmen. Yes, God should be the central person in your ventures. Howbeit, second to Him the ultimate test of whether they will succeed or fail lies in the question of whether your plans are geared towards meeting the needs of the human race.

Work with the person inside of the skin instead of the one that you see at skin level and you will automatically reach the person at skin level. Relate to the needs of the inner person and you will automatically relate to the needs of the outer. To be remembered, you must learn to decentralize self and treat others as if your light shines on them instead of you.

Work adequately or, if necessary, work elaborately, pampering or cuddling self behind the scenes. In the arena of the public, this formula requires that you take second and in some cases, third place or less. For your organization to be remembered, its controllers must put people first and then people will put it first. Through their planning telescope, leaders must be able to see people's needs and the means of meeting them even before the people themselves see them. For people to meet your organization's needs, you must meet their personal needs. This is a scientific law of any organization's survival and success. Any other method is structured backwards and is impractical.

Devise your strategy or plan to saturate people with personal gains and they will pay you the price to get them. To execute this system, you must practice until you become a pro at detecting the things that people truly want to gain. Do your research if you have to. Then you must practice until you become a pro at detecting the things that particular people want to particularly gain. Next you must practice until it becomes normal for you to plan and make your progress by giving people what they want in the process as long as it will, to your knowledge, help instead of harm them. This is a very challenging perspective but it is the ultimate method of planning for perpetual success.

On a terrestrial level, your planning for perpetual success should include the following questions.

Question #1: What areas of human life can you or your organization serve as you plan to launch a new project, make better the existing one or become perpetually successful?

Answer: The answer should be fully known to you, and all those involved in your organization's planning.

Question #2: How can you maximize the human gains or benefits through your project or quest to become perpetually successful within those areas?

Answer: The answer should be fully manifested in the plans made from your planning sessions.

Question #3: How should you go about perfecting the strategies of distributing your cause, while disguising the intent or motive, and at the same time parading the satisfaction or benefits of that product or project?

Answer: This answer should be the silver lining of your plan for perpetual success in anything.

CHAPTER 6
Approach Your Dream Professionally

Take your camera off you and focus it on others for the rest of your life – snap pictures of them instead of you, develop their pictures to their gain, portray those pictures back to their rightful owners and watch the world flock to you for portraits of their pictures.

Professionals have disciplined qualities. A careful analysis of the outstanding people of the world, those who have managed to chart their way to the top, identifies some distinctive qualities about them. They realize that status by possessing and executing qualities that appear to be present in people of similar status all across the world. Whether they are conscious of it or not, the qualities are generally similar in all of these shapers.

They are easy to be drawn to and very easy to love. Others find these people worthy of the leadership role of their lives, and it is sometimes even a pleasure to give them this position. In most

What goes on backstage of the arena of achieving a dream

instances, people voluntarily support them long before they even ask for it. People give them approval and, in many instances, vigorously defend them when others seek to destroy them.

The entire lifestyle of this type of people can be summarized in one concept: *"they are people persons."* They are the people who seek to approve more than condemn. They find it a pleasure to bring out their best by bringing out the best in others. They seem to have grasped the secret of figuring out what people really need and are willing to supply it or help them to achieve it even before they figure it out for themselves.

In their mission and lifestyle, they are able to communicate help to others. They avoid drawing attention to people's shortcomings, they never endeavor to use shortcomings as weapons or to broadcast them publicly. They seek to draw attention to others instead of themselves. They are patient and long-suffering and tend to tolerate more than the normal proportion of error in others.

In the presence of these people, others find comfort, support and the will to achieve. The professional has a *"for you"* spirit instead of an *"at you"* spirit. He strives to praise the best in you rather than raising the red flag on the worst in you. He helps you to grow and develop by raising the roof on your good qualities and actions, instead of calling attention to, and raising the red flag on you for every instance in which you need to grow or develop. He seeks to motivate people by drawing attention to them every time they make progress rather than drawing attention when they don't.

Professional have established policies. Professional people have learned how to turn the light off themselves and shine it on others. As a lifestyle, others are put in the front line instead of them. This seemingly suicidal dive is done by conscious, deliberate choice with no form of reservation or insecurity.

By policy and lifestyle they are very good trainers because they are excellent at bringing out the best in people. By policy, they find it quite normal to bring out the best in themselves by seeking to bring out the best in others.

Professionals have an established policy of dealing with people, including themselves, that applies straight across the board. Though they might be friendly, sympathetic and helpful, this policy still applies to everyone, including you and me.

They are about production as they are about people, instead of production over the well being of human lives and their success. They dare to produce as they dare to protect. They have an innate policy of perceiving every human being as deserving the same valued treatment, without preferring one over the other. They are about the business of minding their own business, which is usually the people's business. This may refer to their customers, employees, subordinates or even just seeing to it that the average person gets the best that he can get. They are usually not conscious of or deeply concerned about the status quo in their effort to achieve or work. They always go the extra mile.

They always maintain a balance. They don't allow themselves or anyone else to push them into exaggeration or extreme behavior.

Professionals suppress the personal and elevate professional interaction. "Personal" is anything that involves self and emotions taking precedence over another person, duty or "workability." The key word for emotions is "feelings" and the key phrases are "I feel" and "I don't feel," without regard, in most instances, for the immediate or long-term consequence or the reality. Some of the ways in which people express their feelings are love, hate, fear, anger, laziness, weakness and energy

What goes on backstage of the arena of achieving a dream or the lack of it.

"Professional" is the regulating of one's personal feelings as necessary to execute, produce or carry out "that which works" towards others or duty and at the suppression or expense of those feelings. Personal is always triggered by "how I feel" while professional is triggered by "knowhow" and "work-ability."

Even though one might coincidentally produce the right or workable action with a personal action, in most cases he is without the knowledge of the procedure needed to duplicate it. In other words, success was a fluke and you would do him a great favor not to ask him to repeat it. The reason is that, nine times out of ten, he has no intellectual knowledge of the right or workable procedure.

With the professional, it's the opposite. The right and workable action is produced by complete intellectual knowledge of what is being done, how it works, and the results that it will bring. He can hit the target again and again, as many times as he wants or is required to. A professional can explain the procedure before executing it, while executing it and after executing it. And he can produce it again, using the identical principles.

Personal is a born quality; professional is a learned quality. There are three basic types of human beings: 1.) personal and private; 2.) professional and private; 3.) professional and public. Most people are personal and private. Some are professional and private. A choice few are professional and public.

See the table that follows to determine where you stand in the area of your professional versus your personal lifestyle. You may need to work on improving the areas that you need to improve.

The Journey of A Dream

Personal Relation	Professional Relation
Focuses on the problems of both his and other people's problems	Focuses on the solutions both to his and other people's problems
Is hung-up on getting without conscious regulation or concern for others	Designs and directs its getting through satisfying others
Glories in its good qualities and others bad qualities	Raises the roof on others' good qualities
Wants without conscious control or concern for others needs	Wants only those things that work with a high level of concern for other people's needs
Conceals other people's good qualities out of a motive of grudge, fear or insecurity	Declares and rejoices in others' good qualities realizing that each of us is different.
Magnifies and encourages destructive criticism by itself and others	Discourages or destroys destructive criticism by itself and others
Asks problem-seeking questions	Asks solution-seeking questions
Asks abortive or stagnating questions	Asks directive, challenging or progressive questions
Asks questions in the negative	Asks questions in the positive
Pursues the direction of the problem	Pursues the direction of the solution
Pursues the direction of dormancy or non-production	Pursues the direction of progress or achieving
Addresses other people with average or demeaning titles	Addresses other people with noble titles (i.e. boss, chief, expert, etc.)
Addresses other people with isolating titles	Addresses other people with associative titles (i.e. my friend, comrade, partner, colleague, etc.)
Investigates to find reasons to disassemble, unscramble, tear apart or destroy	Investigates to find reasons to harmonize, enhance, unify, or strengthen
Is stuck on why did you do it, instead of how can we solve it?	Asks, so what do we do now or how do we solve this issue?
Is exclusive in social interaction	Is inclusive in social interaction

CHAPTER 7
Relate For Success

Be careful whom you ignore! It's a royal art to be silent enough to discern what people are really communicating. What they speak is just a symptom of what they mean. What they mean lies somewhere between what they speak and how they speak it.

Some people, just by the atmosphere that they give off or the general message they express through their behavior, literally kill their support before they gain it. I remind you that you don't necessarily have to say a word to hit this target every time. It can happen just by your demeanor.

It can happen both by your conscious and unconscious behavior. Most importantly, it can happen just by living your life without the principles that counter such a result.

Here is where the real practicality of the journey of your

dream comes in. Here is why many people have stayed hung-up with only a lifetime plan and never reached further than that. They will complete their plan tonight and tomorrow go out and support an ignorant, avoidable psychological battle which cuts off one or more supporters or potential supporters. The same day they pass dozens of people on the streets without hailing them. The same day they pass several people who are kind enough to hail them and they are either so busy or so proud that they choose not to return the hail. This results in the cutting off of a few more supporters. Calculate them doing that every day or every other day. By the time they are finished, they have done a good job of cutting off instead of adding to their supporters.

To truly set the tone for a smoother journey to a dream, you will have to resolve to consciously and deliberately network with people, and dare to carry it out. You should endeavor to live a life of respect for people, even when they choose to do the opposite to you. To pave the way to the journey of your dream, it is required of you, the dreamer, to respect first and also dare to respect last. An ideal principle for setting the stage for a smoother journey to your dream also lies in daring to defend other people first and also daring, to defend them last.

Take stock in people. Fools invest in financial institutions; wise people invest in people. The money in institutions is of no use without their controllers, the people. The people who run those institutions are themselves the real institutions. The best investment of all is into the operators of that which is created, instead of the product or the place of its abode. You have yet to invest until you invest in people. Second to God, it is people who control this planet. Invest in people and you will have invested in yourself because you too are a part of the people.

The following principles are human investments that will bring incalculable returns. They are otherwise known as "professional relating." The most socially economical way to enter a person's heart is to let him let you in: "Be a perpetual contender for being the first to do good to people." The world's people deeply desire it, but our society teaches them to expect the opposite, so surprise them and they'll both thank you and love you for it.

There is no winning without losing and a winner must lose some things to obtain that winning objective. If you want to win people, you must consciously and deliberately lose the substance that they are aspiring to win, and give them the glory that they so desperately crave. To gain even a higher rate of approval, help them to win that precious substance.

Always construct and conclude your statements and conversations making the other person a winner. Seek to let your audience get the last word, or at least feel that it does.

People don't ever intend for their mistakes or flaws to be paraded: "Avoid drawing attention to another person's flaws or mistakes, if you can avoid doing so." Keep the lowest tone possible on a person's mistakes or flaws, including your own. In actuality, the level at which you are hard on yourself, is the level at which you are hard on others. First measure the level at which you will be hard or soft on others by how you are on yourself. Be a social sportsman and catch people's mistakes or flaws before they drop and explode them; smooth them out and credit the act to their pride or self-image. They will love you for it. Seek to praise the person in the direction of recovery instead of affirming the person in the direction of stagnancy.

People who are at a disadvantage want to know more about how they can rise above or get out of their condition or situation instead of being affirmed in their existing condition. In correcting a person, including yourself, "focus on the solutions," and fight the problems with them and for them. Nine times out of ten, if you can simply direct or channel a person to the solutions to his/her struggles and get him/her to focus on and implement the solutions, you will get a better and longer-lasting result than if you had drawn attention to his problems. In most instances, if you focus on the solutions, you will have the other person focusing on the solutions too, or at least you will help him to focus on them.

The following approach exemplifies a more appropriate means of diagnosing the root of a situation: 1.) It is better to ask "what is the situation" rather than "what is the problem?" 2.) "what do we need to address here" rather than "what's wrong? These questions are used to diagnose problems without drawing unnecessary attention to them or focusing on them in an alarming way.

The following approach exemplifies a better and more appropriate way to locate a solution to a particular situation: 1.) "what do you think is the best way to handle the situation" instead of "why did you let this happen?" 2.) "What should we do now to resolve this situation" instead of "why didn't you do this at the time?" These questions get the person thinking and accepting the reality that the situation needs to be, and can be resolved if we start discussing solutions.

The following examples illustrate a better method of applying solutions: 1.) "It would appear that the best deal that we have in this situation is...;" 2.) "If I were you, I would start doing this...;" 3.) "From what I see, it would be in your best interest to do this...;" 4.) "After analyzing the situation, my recommendation is...;" 5.) "The biblical solution is to do this...."

Vision your way into people's hearts: "Make it your mission in life to always look for the good points in people, instead of the bad." People are a pro at identifying the subjects of this course in the human race. "Be looking for things to compliment, instead of to criticize." Every person, regardless of how terrible he/she is, has something that can be complimented. It is always appropriate to compliment. Your last hope for gaining a person's approval is to compliment him/her. Teach your way to a better world: "Teach people of their good qualities..." and they will teach you how aspiring they can be. "Be a fanatic at complimenting instead of criticizing."

Never kill a person's spur to live up to his good qualities. If he chooses to pamper himself or his good qualities to you, pamper them with him, even if it requires you playing a fool to help a fool sometimes.

Meekness is power under control. Distribute authority

What goes on backstage of the arena of achieving a dream appropriately and with "retro-perspective." "Power is demonstrated in showing what you can refrain from doing, instead of what you can do only." A person's submission to you or anyone is no absolute evidence that he couldn't refuse to submit. So be slow to interpret it that way.

Two wrongs never make a right and a gift that is not received is left with its bearer still. "Never wash a dirty product with dirty water or receive a dirty gift from its carrier." Regardless of how much that gift is forced upon you, if you stop short of receiving it, both it and its burden still rest upon its bearer.

Instigate change by taking the initiative to lead a revolution in the right direction. People are easier led into doing the right, than driven. It is easier to get the other person to bow to you by you bowing to him first, than by demanding that he bows to you first. Consciously instigate revolution in the right direction by voluntarily initiating it. Submit or bow to the attention seekers and you will begin the process of a revolution in the right direction and secure the credit for it. Dare to break the cycle of wrong by being the first to start the cycle of right and you will shape history instead of imitating it, plus you will gain the credit for it. Dare to set the standard, to be an inventor instead of a parakeet, and you will gain the credit for it.

Dare to volunteer to give people your sword by its handle before they demand it of you, and in addition to sparing you the blade, they will in turn give you the handles of their swords also. Just holding the blade for a short while may change your mind from delivering it to another person. If you have to deliver it, keep the worst part and give the best. And if you have to give the whole sword, pad the way with the best part first before you deliver the worst. You will have padded the way to accepting the worst. Give the handle before the blade. After giving the rod of correction, counter the act with showers of comfort, love, loving comments and gestures.

Give the person his good points in other areas, confess your shortcomings in the area he is short or another area, then show him a way out.

There are four ways to respond to someone who addresses you: 1.) You can simply allow yourself to hear what is being said but give absolutely no response to indicate approval or disapproval, agreement or disagreement. 2.) You can simply acknowledge what was said without adding to or subtracting from it. In this response, you give some indication, by sound or action to indicate that you understand, though not necessarily agree with or approve of what was said; 3.) You can indicate to the person that you both understand and agree with what was said. The potential for offense is usually absent from this response. 4.) You can indicate to the person that you both understand and disagree with or disapprove of what was said. The potential for offense is usually highly present in this response.

The safest posture for the listener while probing for the speaker in any conversation is no response. By stopping short of a response, whether you approve or disapprove, agree or disagree, you leave the person room to rethink what was said without you exposing your

What goes on backstage of the arena of achieving a dream position. With this response, the person will have nothing to hold you accountable for. The most appropriate and safe response for both the speaker and the listener is to simply acknowledge what was said by indicating understanding in action or sound but stop short of approval or disapproval. Though this response has less room for repercussions to the listener than non-acknowledgment, the person still has no position to hold you accountable for. One of the safest forms of overt disagreement or disapproval and least offensive is to ask questions to cause the person to rethink certainty in his/her position or ask questions to suggest or encourage an alternative.

Never dispose your mental garbage into your neighbor's mind and make not your mind his garbage disposal. The mind that harbors litter is a home-bound garbage bin. If you cannot prevent the other person from disposing his garbage, stop short of inviting him to litter in your mind. As much as possible, think and speak well of all persons... anything else is "mental garbage." If you are unable to stop the other person from doing the other, deliberately stop short of giving a positive response. Defend the victim as much as you can, whether he/she is present or absent, especially if he/she is absent. In the case of an absent victim, the accuser is present to defend himself but he isn't. Never form a conclusion from one side of a story. A story has three sides - your side, my side and the right side. One of the deadliest dilemmas of human relation is the act of conclusion before investigation.

The person who gossips to you will gossip about you 99.9 percent of the times. So when you encourage that person to gossip to you, you are encouraging a habit that will definitely be used as an arson against you at some point. What would you like the other person to do when this deadly form of weaponry is leveled against you to him/her? Do the same when it is being communicated to you. Proverbs sixteen, verses twenty seven through twenty eight says: "An ungodly man diggeth up evil: and in his lips there is as a burning fire. A froward man soweth strife: and a whisperer separateth chief friends."

It's a sure person who says only what he knows. "Practice to say only what you are absolutely sure of. Stop the assuming jungle and the extra ramification. It is no crime to remain silent as you think about the appropriate and/or accurate thing to say or response to give.

The three sweetest sounds to a person's ears are: 1.) their name associated with something prestigious; 2.) "you are right," and 3.) "you win." So, if you want a person to enjoy interacting with you, make it your policy to associate him and his name with the highest level of prestige possible. Be anxious to approve his statements instead of criticizing them and make him the winner in each interaction, as much as you can or at least make him feel that he is.

If you want to be a good leader of followers, first be a good leader to followers. "Volunteer to, and make yourself, be a good follower when it is your duty." A leader is selected; an oppressor is usurped. Remember that you might be there soon.

Can you be a sea? Can you stay lower than your rivers? Can you receive a wealth of water and still keep a low profile? Can you consider depth more precious and valuable than height?

What goes on backstage of the arena of achieving a dream

Regardless of your audience's status, gauge yours lower than theirs and they will be motivated and not be afraid to continue to give you support. Regardless of the quantity of goods that you possess, be and appear reachable and don't ever rise above your support pipeline. Always seek to be inexhaustible in your chosen field. Always seek to develop more and continue to grow in your specific field while maintaining balance.

People don't like to be too familiar with you or anyone, so know and keep your distance with them. "Don't be too present to any one person including your spouse, if you catch my drift." Try your best not to let people say of you, "I-have too-much-of" him/her, in words or in action. That is not a good sign, so don't ever give all of you to any one person, give a portion of you to all persons.

Be a standard-setter. Learn to accept it as normal to initiate the right, instead of imitating. Dare to refuse as much as possible, to react negatively to people's negative actions or reactions; seek to help them react positively to your positive actions and reactions. Resolve to act positively to all negative actions or reactions, and let them so react to you in the long- or short-run.

These are social investments that will bring incalculable long-term or lasting returns. An amazing fact is that people promote your good qualities to their friends, but they also promote your bad. And in most instances, they do a better job of promoting these aspects than you. If you would like to pave the way for an adventurous journey to your dream, you must be skillful in relating to the innermost desires of people, instead of the surface.

Take stock in a process. Be not surprised if you are uniquely isolated when you choose to carry out this kind of lifestyle. Though amazing, it is true that in practicing this portion of your success formula you may have very little, if any, company or competition. Just continue to execute the process. Dare to resolve that this kind of relating is the opposite of a launch into the dark. You know that you are doing it to bring about a particular result. That result will come to you if you consistently and sincerely execute these processes. It might be the opposite of a sudden rush of rewards, but with your standard-setting approach toward living, you will see the fruits of your labor in the process of time. The reality of these strategies is that when they start bearing fruits, it will be long-term, substantial, lasting and rewarding.

Always strive to be first to execute this kind of relation. Do not wait for it to be done to you first and then return it. You must take the first step. Remember that you are a standard-setter, not an imitator.

Be advised that temporary loss isn't absolute evidence of total loss. In practicing this aspect of your success, you might find that others seem to be getting ahead of you in terms of immediate advancements. Your duty is never to worry or be alarmed over that. Just continue to work toward your long-term goals as rewards. Keep reminding yourself that one right, workable and permanent step is far better than one thousand wrong, unworkable and temporary ones. Most importantly, your goal is to capture a long term, wide range and should be characterized by permanency.

What goes on backstage of the arena of achieving a dream

These qualities must genuinely come from you. If you do not already possess the ability to relate to the innermost desires of people, you should find a way to inculcate this skill into your being rather than exercising it as a ritual. It must emerge naturally. This move will be indescribably vital to your continuous success in anything or the successful journey to your dream.

The more you can learn about dealing with people, the better you will be able to practice this portion of your success formula. It is important to note here that second to God, it is people who will make you a success. This includes you. Though often rejected, it is true that the average person loves to follow the crowd, the majority. You will more successfully plant your feet with the crowd supporting you, if you are going to gain the masses' approval. The more of the crowd that you can get to support you before you open your mouth, the more you will be guaranteed successful results when you put down your feet or state your cause. Later we will discuss how to get them to support you.

Again, to continuously pave the way to the journey of your dream, you must plug yourself into your home-based empire, lay a sure foundation for an unlimited, unshakable, and growing project and you must also learn to discern and relate to the innermost desires of people instead of the surface.

CHAPTER 8

Invent As A Lifestyle

Awake the giant in you. Every construction and development on this planet is the child of a mind - either the mind of God or, in a secondary way, a human mind. Such minds can give birth to wondrous children. Has yours given birth to any as yet? If so, how many more can it give birth to?

Which are you, a sluggard or a slick? We have hundreds of potentially "limitless" organizations and many people that have yet to utilize even half their potential in service and/or development. Such utilization would result in an increase of prosperity and much more. The amount of people who remain in a "potential" state, instead of actualizing their abilities is alarming. Whether you are a pastor, president, student, controller, founder, etc., who sits on your bottom and feed off last month's, week's, day's, hour's or even minutes' achievements, you are cheating yourself. You need to put your human computer to work and develop new inventions.

There are those that have multiplex competition and commitments yet are still ranked with those in the top bracket. How did they do it? They invent as a lifestyle. Inventing as a lifestyle means that inventing is a lifetime endeavor. What was done "yester-time" is history. You need to continue to develop. Use your mind to invent what you want to accomplish or better worded, what God is leading you to do, and put the rest of yourself to the task to bring your inventions to fruition.

To successfully travel the journey to your dream, you must: 1.) become a true agent of your future empire; 2.) plan to sail instead of fail; 3.) relate to the deep desires of people; 4.) continuously strive toward higher heights by being a creative person; 5.) invent as a lifestyle, and, as we will see; 6.) complete all of your inventions.

Release the lions from your den. Invention is a four-fold art. You must take the fourth step to completely invent. The first aspect of invention is the process of a searching imagination. This searching imagination involves getting into the mood of invention, researching and investigating the available resources that are crucial to the formulation and construction of your intended invention. The purpose for carrying out this comprehensive research is to ensure that you identify and utilize the best there is available to you. This step should be repeated or implemented until the second stage takes place.

What goes on backstage of the arena of achieving a dream

The second stage of invention is finding a possible idea. The moment you hit the possible idea, you reach the second stage of invention. Your job, immediately, is to get that idea to a place where you do not lose it. The second stage of invention may come after the reading of several books, listening to speakers or watching a movie on the subject. It might come by your own repeated investigative and imaginative sessions. But when you find it, please preserve it!

Many people need to activate or reactivate the second aspect of their success journey. This stage need not have a specific time or place. It could be in the taxi, in the classroom, in bed, around the dinner table, any place and any time but do not, I repeat, do not lose it. Your job is to get it to a place where it is impossible to lose it. You should seek to secure this idea immediately because some thoughts or ideas only pass by once. If you miss it, you lose it for life.

The third stage of invention is designing a plan that will make your possible idea a reality. The best plan is a detailed step-by-step plan that has your entire path mapped out. This portion is self-explanatory. It means just what it says. Make a plan or map out a diagram with the route that you are going to travel to make your priceless idea a reality. The best plan is a detailed step-by-step plan that has your complete path mapped out. Seems like an unconscious repetition? Quite the contrary! This was done deliberately to drive home the importance of a complete plan or diagram. By this time you have a goal, namely to get this idea to become a reality. Remember that one good idea can be worth millions of dollars or can be a priceless addition to your life or organization. The big move is to get that idea to become a complete invention. This task is done by adding the final stage.

Even though the first three stages of invention are very vital and precious even at the moment they occur. Even though it is indescribably satisfying to reach the third stage and to know that there is a way to get your idea to become a reality, you need the fourth and final step to prevent all the others from remaining mere ideas.

Action is the final step of invention. Even though this step is instructional considering that you already have a detailed step-by-step plan, before this step is where most people remain parked. Thousands of people have started to invent great numbers of formulas, have them on the shelf, but have yet to take this step in their invention process. May I say to you that your invention needs just one more step to be completed, *"action."* Although action is ranked fourth in number, it is by no means of lesser importance to the other three steps. It is this step that should be the ultimate focus and destination of any invention. This step is the *"magic step"* of any invention. It puts the magic in the process of any invention. Ignoring or minimizing this step is even more of an automatic sabotage than the other three steps. To ignore or minimize this stage, or any one of the other stages, is to abandon the entire invention.

May I add to this magic step, two prescriptive word-formulas to be used with it for continuous success in any venture? These two prescriptive word-formulas are *"continuous action"* and *"persistent*

What goes on backstage of the arena of achieving a dream action." These two processes, added to the magic word "action," make this step the super step of invention.

CHAPTER 9
Train For Championship

The moment you stop winning, you "WERE" a winner. Can you tell if you are a champion? A careful examination of the people who have charted a path to the top of the ladder, reveals that there are specific qualities about them that bring about such results. The truth is that such status is an acquired one. Though it is dependent upon them not only to possess, but carry out these qualities, if the qualities become absent they would fall back among their average colleagues. The qualities that are found in these distinguished human beings are what make them stand out above the rest. What are these qualities? How do they differ from those who are just survivors? What keeps them going, and going above the rest?

One of the top qualities that is very evident in true champions is that they dare to involve their entire selves and more in what they are doing. If they are doing a project or venture, one hundred percent plus of them is there. It is in them to give all that they can to their particular cause and reach as high as they can in their particular devotion. They elaborately apply themselves to explore deeper depths and higher heights in what they have set out to do in their specific field. They are very generous with their time and the resources required to be more than average in their specific devotion. Since they have given so much of themselves, it is normal for them to operate above the status quo. Their policy is to go the extra mile, two extra miles and more. Another quality that is found in all true champions is that they are standard-setters. They dare to break the previous record, rise above the average, establish new records and implement methods that are different from those currently in place. In many instances, the efforts and resources that they give to their particular cause are available to all of their colleagues. What makes the difference in the people with championship qualities is that they are the ones who dare to apply them. In most, and quite possibly all instances, the application of those qualities is the only difference between the champions and the non-champions.

    One of the fearful realities about championship status is that, to keep that status, you have to constantly maintain those qualities that got you there. The moment you stop winning, you were a winner. This is why it is better to own these qualities than to produce them for temporary exhibitions. The true champion both owns and executes these qualities throughout his lifetime. The true champion owns these qualities and is these qualities. When others think of you, they should have no problem equating those qualities with you. Conversely, they should have a problem thinking of you without those qualities that got you there.

Another outstanding quality that comprises the lifestyle of a champion is that his training is a permanent routine. A champion knows that seasoned preparation is worth much more than an overnight cram, so he constantly keeps in shape even when there is no immediate contest. The truth is that even though a champion has no immediate contest, he always expects one.

Winning is only a secondary objective to the champion. The primary objective for a champion is to top or exhaust his potential and execute his skills at top performance. Whenever he accomplishes that, he has proven himself to be in the best shape that he can. If you train to top your potential, you will be in your best shape to take on any contest.

A true champion keeps on practicing even when the crowd stops. A champion dares to practice in public if he has to, and he keeps on practicing even when he is left by himself to pass or fail the real test of championship. He practices when there is applause and recognition and practices with even greater intensity when there is no one to applaud.

The true champion practices when there are unavoidable results and he keeps doing so when there are little or no visible results. The fact that results are not visible at a particular interval is not necessarily accurate evidence that the method, strategy or application isn't working. It could simply mean that the application is working internally, going through its proper channels or taking the required amount of transitional time. When the doctor prescribes a particular medicine for the body, do you always see visible results immediately or how it is working before its time?

The true champion makes it a matter of duty to walk away from the biggest or most enticing attractions because of his commitment to his necessary practice time. He will practice in spite of, or in the midst of, intense attraction. Right in the midst of the crowd, celebration or parade, he will switch gears to his practice or walk away to get his practice in, regardless of who it hurts or how enjoyable the procession may be.

These principles of preparation and practice are the same principles behind performance and production. The key command in practice and preparation is, "execute the process every time, throughout its entirety," and the same is the command in performance and production.

Since you want to see results, "execute the process!" When you receive recognition and applause, "execute the process!" When you do not get any recognition or applause, "execute the process!" When you see obvious results, "execute the process!" When you or anyone else cannot see the immediate results, "execute the process," until you have convincing evidence that it has stopped working or does not work at all.

It might surprise you one day. Out of the arena of faithfulness, determination, persistence and effective execution of the process, when you least expect it, you may see results so overwhelming that you cannot avoid being recognized and rewarded. When you take inventory you may discover that you have suddenly become a star in a large realm, you have actually broken your bars of enclosure, your payday has finally come and you have actually won your war! You take another survey and it finally dawns on you that you rightfully are seated on the throne that you have worked so long and tiresomely for, that you are wearing the crown that was yours all along, that your success is beyond the reach that you even can touch, that, indeed, a new day has come. Then you realize that it is all there, right in front of you, like it had been placed on a silver platter, just for you.

In actuality, success is placed on your silver platter because you put it there. It is placed there because you have paid for it with your own sweat, substance, self and the help of the Almighty God. It is placed there because you have diligently earned it with your every resources instead of receiving it as a gift. You now own it because you earned it.

Another vital quality that makes up the lifestyle of a champion is that he commits to worthy challenges. In the first place, a champion is a champion because he has earned his way there. He has tackled the odds and proven himself above them all - the best. He has come out head and shoulders above those odds to deserve a reward rather than a gift; he earned his crown! The best way I know to illustrate this truth is by using a statement that was made to describe the struggle of the black person in America: "Whites get breaks but blacks make breaks." This means, of course, that while whites are given advantages, blacks must create theirs against the odds.

A champion knows that the moment that he stops winning, he was a winner. Therefore, to continue to prove that he still is a winner, he continues to tackle the existing odds. A true champion has learned that to keep his crown, he must continue to execute the qualities that gained him the crown in the first place. He accepts this truth irrespective of the crown that he may presently possess. He continues to produce because he is always prepared to prove to himself and the public whether or not he's a champion. In actuality, whether he can still execute the qualities that worked for him in the past is a chance that he is always willing to take.

Another outstanding quality of a champion is that he fights to win throughout the entire contest. In the first place, he fights to win even when no one else is doing so. A true champion, who became one through means other than a fluke or coincidence, finds it both normal and delightful to stay ahead of the game. Instead of limiting the level of his skills to that of his surroundings or how others are executing their skills, he/she is always an *"all-I-can-get-done person."* Instead of doing enough just to come out safe or unhurt, a champion does whatever is necessary to win or be the best that he can.

One of the big differences between a champion and a survivor is that a survivor is satisfied with fighting to a draw or a loss as long as he comes out safe, but a champion wants to know that, on the scoring system, he is registered at the top. Therefore, it is normal for him both to be ahead and to delight in doing so if it's the result of doing his best. He seeks to avoid the risk of someone else fighting to win without him knowing, so he fights to win, always.

A declaration often made by many boxing champions that fits this principle is this: "Even though this is not a championship fight, I am not taking him lightly. I am going to fight him as if I were fighting a championship fight."

One of the greatest pound-for-pound heavyweight boxing champions of the world made a statement after one of his most momentous victories which drove home the point under discussion. After Iron Mike Tyson won his victory over the then W.B.C. World Heavyweight Champion James Bruno on Saturday, March 16, 1996, his words were, *"I'll fight anyone and I still have some improvement to do. I am still not at my best yet."*

At that time, Iron Mike Tyson had just fought his way through one of the most turbulent convictions and jail terms. He had fought and won one other fighter before his Bruno heavyweight fight. On that date, March 16, 1996, he was victorious again. Do you see why he has been so victorious through the years?

A true champion fights to win both when he has a worthy or seemingly unworthy opponent. If there is one thing that should be remembered about a champion, it is that his aim is to be his best and to perform at that level. If it results in him being far ahead on the scoring card, it's not his duty to apologize for the results. And this instance is no exception.

What goes on backstage of the arena of achieving a dream

Does a champion panic when he has a worthy opponent? The opposite is true; he seeks to be in full control of himself and his skills. At this point, he still focuses on executing the process of his skills with deliberate, calculated, regulated actions and control. A champion acts instead of reacts.

A champion fights to win, even after experiencing casualties or hurt. The average fighter fights to win before experiencing casualties, after that, he fights to survive. The champion is different. He fights to win throughout the entire fight. Some fighters need to remember that being in a fight means hurt is highly possible, even severe hurt. This should never take a fighter by so much surprise that he loses control and the will to win.

So you survived? Are you really a survivor? How far do you go in your efforts? Is "the status quo" your motto in life? Are you satisfied with enough, or do you keep on going beyond enough? Is risk a no-no for you and safety your abode? Is getting there just on time satisfactory or getting there in time to sit down and wait, your policy?

One of the outstanding qualities that characterizes a survivor's lifestyle is that he trains or practices only when he has an exhibition in view, regardless of whether it is sufficient or not. The survivor only performs out of obligation so he trains or practices out of obligation also. The survivor's philosophy is to do just what is necessary to survive. Therefore, it is the method that he produces in his preparation and production. He will try to do a lot in a very short period of time not necessarily to maximize his productivity or improve, but because he has to get it done within the little time he has left to do so.

He is also a last-minute person. He will wait until he cannot go on waiting any longer to start his chores. In short, he is a procrastinator. He is a short-term sower. He will do just enough to get him by this time and the same the next time. Very rarely will he do enough to get him beyond one performance. Surplus is a never-land for the survivor. His storehouse is rarely necessary, and if at all, never for long. It is often dry. His motto is "enough" and, "as needed," is his method. If, by chance, the storehouse gets some extras, he sees no need to put out anymore effort until the stock in his storehouse is exhausted.

Another outstanding quality that makes up the lifestyle of the survivor is that he performs only because he cannot avoid a performance. There are two basic reasons why one seeks to avoid an exhibition: confidence and lack of confidence or fear. One is confident in his skills to such an extent that he is fearful of hurting the opponent. The other lacks confidence in his skills to such an extent that he is fearful of hurting himself or being hurt. One is confident in self-skill or knowledge, the other is confident in the opponent's skills or knowledge.

Self-confidence comes by strong belief in the "work-ability" of the knowledge or skills that one possesses a high level of familiarity with them and a fluent form of executing them. A very good example of this is the martial arts. One of its philosophies is that you learn its art not to fight but to avoid a fight, in that, it is so dangerous that you should try your utmost never to use it on anyone. The reason for avoiding a fight in this case is way above the lack of confidence in one's skills. It is a super strong confidence in its effectiveness.

Lack of confidence comes by disbelief in the "work-ability" or effectiveness of the skills that one possesses. One is afraid of losing so he tries to avoid having to perform. This is the class that the survivor falls in. And this lack of confidence or fear can make that person very dangerous if he has to perform. Since he lacks the confidence in his skills or knowledge, he is going to try his utmost to out your lights in one shot so that you do not get to execute your weaponry which he believes is more effective than his. And believe me, he might just succeed. If that happens, it would not be because he was performing to win, but to save his head, to survive or to prevent himself from being hurt, safety only.

The survivor may perform in an exhibition which he couldn't avoid and may very well perform exceptionally to the point of winning. At the same time, he would have performed exceptionally just to avoid being hurt instead of proudly executing the skills that he possesses and is proud of.

CHAPTER 10

Congratulations! You Have Struck Gold!

Who controls your gold? Take human support away from any one person and extinction is his destination. Without support, you are like a traveler in a mad world with an arsenal of deadly weapons pointed at your head with everyone saying, "Freeze!"

You could be the richest or most independent person who ever lived, you are frozen without the support of other people. That's as indisputable as one and one equal two, and as the law of gravity. Do not let even your own mind fool you into believing anything else in the arena of your success. Anything other than this is just fantasy - unrealistic and impractical.

Every person or organization requires the support of other people to get anywhere, to do anything. The businessperson who has, or is going to own, a potentially international business, has to continuously go through the processes of recruiting the support of other people.

The Journey of A Dream

The pastor who has or will have a church that will become worldwide in service, has to go through the processes of recruiting other people's support for his cause. We could go on and on with organizations and people that have been, are, or will be successful, and if you are wondering what their secrets are, one of them is a continuous recruiting of the support of others.

Have you ever stopped to wonder who is sub-ruling the earth? I say "sub," because the ultimate ruler of this earth is God Himself. By Him, the universe is held together, the scripture says. The sub-rulers of the earth are none other than people like you and me. Second to God, it is people who will make you or break you. You have to deal with them day after day. You might as well realize and accept the fact that you are already a creature of an earth that is full of people or people-oriented beings like yourself. Check and see how far you can travel before coming into contact with another creature like yourself. Really try it and see. Like the fish has to live in the sea full of fishes and other sea creatures like itself, so you and I have to live on the earth full of people and people-oriented creatures like ourselves. Why not switch places with the fish... you might seriously want to do that if you choose not to effectively acknowledge the validity of the role of people in your existence and success. You can survive among them, through them and by them but never without them. You might as well start seeing them as creatures equally worthy of this earth just as you and I are.

Take a little time to notice something else. Take a visual tour of the organizations and institutions of any time period or dispensation and see who controls them, who support them. You could learn a lesson that **you** might well have overlooked before you realized *"US."* We control

What goes on backstage of the arena of achieving a dream

your institutions. We control our institutions. We control all institutions or at least sub-control them.

We make the stars stars. We make the products bestsellers. We make the businesses prosperous. We make the schools worth having. We make churches worth keeping. We are present at sports games to make them worth their time. We give organizations reasons to exist. And don't pierce yourself by trying to disregard this truth.

Picture an exhibition that you produced with a lot of your resources, time and efforts. Picture yourself a little further, bringing it to the public with your highest level of expectation and only Mr. Donkey, Miss Cow and Mr. Pig show up. Imagine the high level of support that you would have been given and the great measure of returns that you could expect for your efforts. Don't fool yourself or allow others to fool you into believing that people (we) are not the core of your organizations, my organizations or their organizations. There is no organization or institution without us. We have the key to make them or break them. There is no movie without someone making it and others going to watch it, people. There is no selling without salespersons and buyers, people. There are no businesses without inside and outside supporters, people. There are no schools without teachers, administrators and students, people. There are no churches without preachers and members, in fact, the church is the people. There are no sports or games without players and spectators, people. Again my friend, there is none of what you have built or are venturing to build without people… you, me, the movers and shapers. So, in your quest to be successful in anything, you must not and cannot disregard the importance of the support of other people.

The Journey of A Dream

Why look for gold if you don't know what gold looks like? According to Nelson's Dictionary, support is *"that which bears you up; that which keeps you from falling; that which gives necessaries to; help; sustenance."* These are all strong terminologies. What I would like you to do for yourself is to start taking a serious inventory of such entities around you. Do this if you are sitting, starting from a chair or any object you sit on; if you are standing, starting from the flooring that you stand on; if you are lying, starting with the object that you are lying on. Don't lean, you may find that a wall is bearing you up. Anything or everything that bears you up is support. Right from the outset, consider the fact that they are constructed by people other than God. It is one thing to be living among these things, but it is another to be conscious of them.

Are you beginning to see that you cannot live without support? Hold it! You are not finished as yet. You have a lot more things to name so "just keep on going." Eliminate some more things. It won't be long before you have to start taking out the place that your feet are connected to. That is support. Do you get the point? You need to read the previous paragraph again if you didn't. Your success in anything depends on how conscious you are of this reality. Those of you who live and move in vehicles, don't get in your cars… they are also means of support.

By "that which bears you up" I am referring to factors that are both physical and beyond physical boundaries. Physical support would also refer to the food that you eat which was farmed by people. However, I am also talking about all other areas in which you are borne up, including your social life, your spiritual life, your emotional life, your

What goes on backstage of the arena of achieving a dream

moral life, your financial life, etc.

Remember that we still have the other aspects of the support definition to look at. Can you think of anything or anyone that keeps you from falling? What about that which is giving you your necessities? Can you think of anything or anyone that is helping you? You also have the aspect of sustenance to look at. If you are unable to complete your assignment just take it from me as I have done mine very well - you cannot live without support.

Your second assignment is to go over those you have managed to name and see how many of them came from you or from within you. You will make another shocking discovery. Ninety percent of your support comes from without. The outside sources are God, mankind and the other creatures that God made. The other one percent comes from you, and remember that you are a person too.

The moment one starts moving out of the physical realm of support, he begins to see how much he has to depend on the support of other people. Not only can you not live without support, but to put it bluntly, you cannot live without the support of other people. Face this reality head on. Strive on it. Chew it up and swallow it. Digest it well because your life depends on it and your success in anything depends on how much you live like it.

Support means different things to different people. What you or your organization is in need of is support for you. If support is *that which bears you up, that which keeps you from falling, that which provides necessities, help or sustenance*, you must quickly realize that neither you nor your organization can survive without it. Therefore, treat people like that. They are the sub-source of your support, second to God. All your secrets, techniques and strategies should ultimately be aimed at gaining support. Technically, your ultimate objective should be to seek support instead of supporters. *You should know what you are looking for in your supporters and zero in on that substance specifically.* After you get the support from a person that person automatically becomes your supporter, initially. Then your duty towards him or her is to treat him or her like family, a friend, a member of the club.

With support, you concentrate on how to get it., with supporters, you concentrate on how to treat them. Supporters in this instance, refer both to inside and outside supporters.

CHAPTER 11

Preserve Your Mines, Enjoy The Gold

The best formula for killing a tree is to kill its roots: If you kill your supporters your support is dead. Did you think of that? If you treat your supporters with kid gloves, you preserve your support. Of course, if you treat them nastily, it's equivalent to throwing dirt into the bucket that you are drinking from. After God, the best medium for making a famous person or organization is people; "supporters."

Supporters are those who contribute to you or your organization. They are the source of your support. In short, they are those behind your support. Therefore, be warned that if you lose a supporter, you lose his support. Supporters are the fountainheads of your organization, not its exhaust pipes.

Keep in mind that money is only one form of support that a person can contribute to your cause. Money is an exclusive form of support only if that's all that you or your organization is in need of at any given time. A supporter can be contributing more than one source of support to you or your organization. For example, a supporter can be contributing his presence, his services, his money, his encouragement and his good recommendation to your organization. It is more than important to treat this supporter very well.

There are actually three basic kinds of supporters. There are inside supporters, outside supporters and prospective supporters. The inside supporters are those inside your organization serving the outside supporters. They are those who keep records, help to make decisions, keep your organization in an acceptable and comfortable state for your outside supporters. They accept the goals and objectives of your cause or organization as theirs and are working toward them along with you. They express an honest feeling of understanding and sympathy when needed.

The outside supporters are those who actually contribute to your cause or organization, but are outside the administrative or service aspect of it. They are served by your organization but are not responsible to serve in it. They are also as important as the inside supporters.

If you treat the inside supporters with kid gloves, it will project to your outside supporters. The way to really reach your outside supporters is to reach your inside supporters, including yourself. The first and last image that your outside supporters get from your organization is what your inside supporters give them. If your inside supporters are happy, they will make your outside supporters happy. If the opposite is true, it will almost always be apparent to your outside supporters.

The third kind of supporters are your prospective supporters. Prospective supporters are all human beings. Everyone who is not yet contributing to your cause or organization or can increase or expand their support is a prospective supporter. The more that you are able to view people this way, the more you will see the need to relate to the innermost desires of people. With this perspective on life, you will find yourself, through conscious efforts, tenderly and lovingly dealing with people because you will realize their importance.

Dig up your gold! Are bees attracted to flowers because of their beauty or their pollen or nectar? There is an international secret used consciously or unconsciously to recruit the support of other people. This secret has maintained a 100 percent success average, the highest of its kind. It is used by every businessperson, every politician, every pastor, every president, every founder and everyone else, consciously or unconsciously, who is greatly successful in gaining support for his/her cause.

This valuable secret is universal in its appeal. Just as magnet naturally attracts every piece of steel regardless of looks, size or origin, so this secret attracts every human being, regardless of his looks, size, origin or present state.

Are you ready for it? It is so simple that you might not even recognize it, but it is very effective. It is none other than "benefits."

What goes on backstage of the arena of achieving a dream

Do not get upset, just keep reading. You have a great deal more to learn about this seemingly insignificant secret.

The undisputed magnet of all human actions is rooted in the desire for benefits - just benefits and more of them! All human acts are founded on one of two earth-shaking principles: love or fear, to get or to get away from. This principle is the rudder of all human action.

In order to motivate someone, you must either get him to love something or get him to fear it's opposite. This is basic, scientific and practical. This is mathematical and there is no way that anyone can successfully get around it. All else is folly and goes against the laws of human movement, unscientific, impractical and only a waste of your precious time. For people to ever budge to help or support you or your cause, it must be saturated with benefits. The more that you or your organization is saturated with benefits, the more people will support it. You say, "This is so old and well known, it has no effect today." Yes, that is partly true, it is old. Yet it is as effective today as if it were invented yesterday. It is not limited by time boundaries. It is well-known by many, yet its effect is often unconsciously overlooked while working. Even though it is sometimes noticed, it cannot be helped. Sometimes when noticed by its objects, a great quantity of its substance is requested. That is how powerful, essential, and effective this secret is.

Every action that a person takes, every movement that person makes, is triggered by his or her desire for benefits. People love because in loving they experience or expect great benefits. It might only be emotional satisfaction, but that is a great benefit. People work because it results in great benefits. They might stick around only for the money's sake, but that is a great benefit. People give because they believe that they will receive benefits. It might only be the returning of gifts, or possible return at a later date, but even that is a benefit in return. People sell because they believe that they will receive benefits from doing so. It might only be money, but even that is a benefit. People buy because of their benefits. It might be just to get you off their backs, but may I say that rest is a great benefit. People follow you because they see in you the possibility, and most likely a great possibility of receiving some benefits. It might only be the thought of receiving freedom or a better life, but that is a benefit and a great one too.

Therefore, to be successful in anything, you, your organization or cause must be saturated with benefits for people, not for any other creature. If you are running an organization that is already started, to be successful it must be saturated with benefits for people. The more, the merrier.

Do your prospects have equal choices? Can you compete in quantity; can you add a little more to your pack than your competition is offering? Remember that the average human being goes wild about numbers; quantity.

Are you unable to compete in quantity? Can you add a greater variety? Can you offer at least one other benefit that your competition does not have? Even a smaller amount of what your competition offers plus one or more other benefits is a plus.

What goes on backstage of the arena of achieving a dream

Can you compete in quality? Can you focus on value and/or durability? Quantity is numerable, but quality is durable. Quantity takes up space, but quality may never be erased.

Attractive future benefits shadow today's standard ones. Do not be completely discouraged if you don't have all of your pack together today. You can present logical and viable evidence that more benefits are coming. The world's people are traveling to tomorrow. I am positive that some would consider it if you present a logical and viable way of receiving a portion of their pack tomorrow with a greater amount of benefits than they are receiving today. How would you react if I promised you a greater quantity, better quality or a greater variety of what your today's pack contains to be delivered tomorrow and guarantee you that it would be worth the wait with a bonus for waiting? Would you at least consider it? I am sure you would. Do you see what I'm saying? So take heart even if you only have a portion or none of your pack today.

CHAPTER 12
Take Five Steps To Harvest

Even though a gun is a very effective protective weapon, the best way to use it is with its know-how because it can destroy you.

Even though you know that the secret that convinces people to support you is "benefits," to use it properly and move from one right point to another, you must know how to use it. Lets examine five basic steps that should minimize the potential for a negative usage of benefits to gain your support. They are as follows.

Step one is to Identify and make clear to yourself and the inside supporters of your cause or organization the existing benefits to people, primarily your target audience. If you or the members of your organization are going to be able to present its benefits effectively to prospective supporters, the benefits have to be very clear to both of you.

To be able to draw people's attention and get them to take action by using your product or participating in your project, you must present their benefits with a high level of knowledge and enthusiasm. To do this, you have to be the first ones to not only identify the existing benefits but you and all who are involved must be sold on your cause. The level at which you are sold on the effectiveness and benefits of your cause is the level at which you will be able to present it to your prospective supporters and furthermore, sell them on it.

You must know your product or project inside out. You must be fully knowledgeable of the areas of need that it can meet. With this knowledge, instead of just listing the benefits that it offers to your intended audience, you can effectively direct these benefits to particular areas of their need or lack.

Step two is to make the existing benefits of your cause visible to people, your prospective supporters. You can rant and rave or kick and stomp all you want, but unless the benefits of your cause are made visible to your intended audience, no one will even budge toward it. That is as factual and practical as one and one equal two.

Think of the last movement that you made towards something or your last attempt to get away from something. See why you did it. Whether you did it to obtain or to escape, your motive was to receive benefits that you perceived as attainable by carrying out such actions. Whether you are conscious of it or not, you wouldn't have moved one muscle unless you clearly saw the possibility of receiving some kind of benefit. Every movement that people make is because they see the possibility of receiving benefits.

Whatever medium you can use to make visible the existing benefits of your cause, you should dare to jump for it. Get the benefits in front of people's eyes... get people to see them by one means or another. Get them in their mouths... get them to taste them and experience the satisfaction that they give. Get them in their entire surroundings so that people will depend on these benefits. Get them everywhere that you possibly can and get people to strive for them.

Step three is to *emphasize and re-emphasize the existing benefits of your cause* to your prospective supporters. In most cases, making visible the existing benefits of your cause the first time will only raise the curiosity of your prospective supporters, and, by itself, will very rarely lead them to buy or claim your cause. Then you will need this other **step**, and that is to *emphasize and reemphasize the existing benefits of your cause* to your prospective supporters.

In this step, your duty is to see that they notice these benefits. This is the only way that they are going to be drawn to take note of your cause. In doing this, you can make them aware of their present state - which many people are not aware of; point out the lack in remaining in that state, show them the benefits of getting out by using your cause, product or project.

You can approach it from a purely comparative point of view. You can compare your cause, product or project with their alternatives... point out the differences and show them the benefits of yours over the others. It is most effective if you seek to offer them your cause while they are in the existing cause. Most people are already involved with a cause. To wait until they are completely free is probably an impossible wait because when people are accustomed to, and are dependent on a particular way of life, they don't usually break away from it without a viably working alternative.

In most or all instances that you make visible or emphasize the existing benefits of your cause to people, you should seek to provide a way or means for them to claim, own or get involved with your cause immediately or as soon as possible. Many people might be willing to take action immediately, but if there are no means of doing so, they are forced to remain with their existing cause. A loss of opportunity could result in a resolve to remain permanently in the existing cause.

In both cases presented above, you can demonstrate them either by your actions, verbally or by visual presentation. Possibly the single most effective means of winning people to your cause is by demonstrating the work-ability of it by living it yourself in front of their eyes. When you make it a lifestyle, you have no problem presenting it verbally or visually with meaning and conviction. You have tested it and seen it work over and over again. It has not only become something that you know or own but it has become you.

Step four is activating a constant reminder of your cause and its existing benefits to your prospective supporters. In many cases, the previous steps will stop short off finishing the job of gaining support because other activities have knocked out the importance of your cause and its benefits. Then you will need this step. It is a constant reminder of your cause and its benefits.

Surprising but true, many people are faithful in the other steps but need to be as faithful in this step also. To prevent failure at this step, it is advisable to make it a lifestyle. By this I mean to do it as often as possible whether by action, visually or verbally.

If you sent a note before, send a note again. If you told them about it before, tell them again. If you showed them before, show them again.

What goes on backstage of the arena of achieving a dream

You can carry out your perpetual reminder by any of the following mediums: 1.) set a calendar sequence of reminders; 2.) set an eventual sequence of reminders; 3.) set a random sequence of reminders and 4.) remind upon every contact or opportunity.

In the "calendar sequence" of reminders, you set up a specific date and/or time on a yearly, monthly, weekly or daily basis to remind your prospects of your cause and its benefits. You can do this by sending out a letter or printed advertisement, having a radio or television broadcast or making a telephone reminder every time the date or time comes around. The "eventual sequence" of reminders is that which is carried out, at, before or after a specific or symbolic event. This means that you do it very time that this event takes place just before or thereafter. Technology is so advanced today that this can be easily automated. Right before, after or at this event, your cause and its benefits are set up to remind your prospective supporters that they should consider taking action on your offer. This method is used when a specific company sponsors the Super Bowl or the Tour de France every year. You can select an event that is already set up and has been ongoing or you can start or create an event.

"Randomly reminders" mean that no specific time or event is required to offset the reminder of your cause and its benefits to your prospective supporters. It could happen anytime during the year, month, week, day or hour. The audience can be prepared to look for it at anytime or you can just surprise them. It could be in the form of a contest that you set up or you could just bring it up at anytime, anywhere that is appropriate.

"At every opportunity" means exactly what it says. Every contact is an opportunity to present your cause and its benefits. With this method of reminder, you find a way to bring it up, whether verbally, visually or by action, every time that contact is made. With this means of reminder, it is within policy to remind upon every approach and to remind upon every departure.

Step five is to skillfully call for the support. In most cases, the previous steps will need one final and most important step. This is to "simply call for the support". Thousands of people still need to acquire the support of others because they haven't yet applied this final step, namely, "asking for it." After you have taken all the other steps, your final and easiest, though most delicate, step is to call for the support.

It would be rather disappointing to reach this far, after putting much effort into the previous processes, only to fail when it could have been avoided. Don't fool yourself into believing that it is hard or impossible to happen. It can happen and is relatively easy at this final step, if done without the following minor precautions.

The first of these, to be applied in calling for support, is *cautiousness*. This is a very important factor in calling for support for your cause. You should realize that it is not worth blowing the deal at this point. It can result in permanent rejection of you and your cause. Moreover, your time would have been wasted. Therefore, you can rarely be too cautious at this juncture. Another word for cautiousness is *sensitivity*. Being sensitive to the other person's feelings, views, goals and being careful not to hurt them unnecessarily, are requirements in calling for support. In fact, if you can appease their concerns first, you will have gotten them out of the way and be on your way to gaining the support you need.

Next, be courteous. *Courteousness is a verbal or non-verbal communication of respect and honor* that is residing within for another person. The theme word for courteousness is *respect* or *honor*. And the magic is showing the respect. This you can actively show verbally, or passively show non-verbally, by fixing your mind in a state of respect for your prospective supporters. Let your negotiation or interaction throughout the entire process be seasoned with it.

You must also be *firm*. Be cautious, be courteous, but be firm. What is meant by being firm in calling for support? First of all, firmness doesn't mean a closed ear, even though this might sometimes be necessary. Neither does it mean closed reasoning power even though this might be necessary sometimes. What firmness does mean is *a super-strong belief in the "work-ability" of your cause and a fearlessly positive and solid demonstration of it.* You also need to believe that it is the best workable solution, or at least, one of the best. You might as well forget it, if you approach it without this concept. With any other approach, you would have already programmed yourself to fail in gaining other people's support. If you don't believe in it, what makes you think that others should?

Finally, "make the way clear and easy" for your prospective supporters to vote or take action. To clear the way means that you should clear every obstacle out of the way and leave only your cause, the need for supporting it, the urgency of doing so, and the opportunity to take action. This is called *"the support block."*

In making it easy to vote or take action on your cause, you might have to do almost all the work. In this segment, it is advisable to leave it where the prospective supporters only oblige you in voting or taking action. For example, a salesman might have to 1.) go to the person's home, 2.) present his product, project or proposal, 3.) take all the necessary processing documents, 4.) obtain the necessary information from the person, 5.) fill out the application, except the signature, 6.) put it in an envelope, 7.) put a stamp on the envelope and 8.) mail the package for the client. A politician might have to 1.) give his speech seasoned with benefits, 2.) clear away all the obstacles and 3.) provide transportation for the person, just to come and give his support. A preacher may have to do the same.

CHAPTER 13

Remove The Snakes From Your Grass

If your cause lies directly west, you are off course if you are traveling northwest. Every winner is a loser and every loser is a winner. Every winner must lose some things to win something, and every loser must win some things to lose something. It is totally up to him to choose what he wants to lose and what he wants to win.

The act of separating yourself from the obstacles of your cause, or, the obstacles of your cause from you is an art. This art is very credible and miraculous, but valueless unless executed. To be fully committed for continuous success in anything, you must go through the process of separating yourself from the obstacles of your cause, or the obstacles of your cause from you. There might be things that are attractive to the eyes, delightful to the body, delicious to the taste, comforting for self-gratification, pleasing to the mind, etc., but if they are obstacles, you must separate them from yourself or yourself from them. You must first separate yourself from the obstacles of your cause before you can be effectively devoted to your cause.

The first separation that you make from any obstacle of your cause is a symbolic measurement of your capabilities which can either be repeated or increased. You will never feel the same after you separate yourself from your first obstacle. You will feel like a victor and, in truth, you are. The real challenge after that is done is to demonstrate to yourself and the world that you can continue to be victorious over more of your obstacles instead of just being victorious over that specific obstacle. Then you would have been on your way to being a victor over all of your obstacles. What are obstacles? Obstacles are anything or anyone that prevents one from going further towards his intended direction or destination. Most likely, one has to stay behind the obstacles for as long as they are still in the way.

Break your seals! The first type of obstacle that we will look at is what I call "inbound obstacles." With this type of obstacles you are bound in and need to overcome your bounds. This may require a high level of wit to overcome, but involves very little or no great risk. For example, a person is in a car that is completely closed or locked up and wants to get into his house that is completely locked up also. The ultimate goal of this person is to get into the house. His obstacles to overcome would be, first of all (and first to be considered), the doors of the car and then the doors of the house. To get into the house, these obstacles must be moved out of the way. No bodily torture or risk is necessarily involved or required. His only requirements are to unlock the doors of the vehicle, get out of the vehicle, unlock the door of the house and get into the house.

Count your casualties. Let's look at another type of obstacle. This is the sacrificial obstacle. This obstacle, like the inbound obstacle, involves wit to remove or overcome but also may involve pain, bodily risk or sacrifice. For example a person is locked up in the same car, rain is falling and he wants to get into his house which is also locked. He, at this point, has in his way more obstacles than just the doors. He now has the rain as his obstacle also. In this case, he cannot move the rain out of the way, so he must either devise a protective method, or go through the rain and get wet if he is going to get into his house. In this case, we see that there will be some obstacles that we cannot move out of our way, but we must either devise a way to protect ourselves through the fiery period until we reach our goals, or go through it and endure the consequence. But be encouraged that if and when you finally reach your goal, it will be a happy and satisfying moment of achievement.

Let's take another type of obstacle. This is the habitual obstacle. This is when an habitual or physical obstacle is present that is getting in the way of you reaching your dream. These you might not be able to separate yourself from, but you can, and must, separate them from you. These kinds of obstacles might be the hardest to get rid of, but if you are going to reach your goal you must, again I repeat, you must get rid of them. The beginning process of getting rid of this kind of obstacle might be very painful, as well as the entire process, but it cannot be compared with the satisfaction and progress that come with complete victory over the obstacle or obstacles.

This kind of obstacle is found also in the absence of certain characteristics that are required to reach your dream as a result of a trait

What goes on backstage of the arena of achieving a dream that prevents those characteristics from being present in your lifestyle. The most prominent of these is laziness, which, when it is present, spells the absence of the motivation or drive to achieve your dream. Habitual or physical obstacles will make you do things that prevent you from reaching your destination and also prevent you from doing the things that are required to reaching your destination. So take a two-way inventory. If they are goal or destination, regardless of what angle they come from, they accomplish the same thing.

Every winner loses. Greed is the next type of obstacle we will look at. It is allowing yourself to be distracted or, worse yet, sidetracked from your aspired goal by an attraction that is not in context with your projected destination. Take warning: whatever you or anyone else does in life's journey, he is a loser, and whatever you or anyone else does in life's journey, he is a winner. Sounds like a contradiction? If it is, it's in sound only. It is perfectly scientific, mathematical and harmonious. Believe me, everything that you lose, someone else wants to win, and everything you win, someone else wants to lose. Therefore what you win is only what your mind is educated to count as winning; and what you lose is also what it is educated to count as losing.

For example, someone might coax himself into eating excess food, regardless of whether he gets fat or not. That is what his mind counts as winning. And, according to his frame of mind and within the sects of such thinking, he most certainly has won and thus a solid winner. But he is also a loser in that he has lost the rewards of moderation and the prevention of getting fat.

On the other hand, another person might choose to eat a moderate amount of food to prevent himself from getting fat and to stay within moderation. That is what his mind is educated to count as winning. Believe it or not, he is also a solid winner and, to the same degree as the other, a perfect loser in that he lost the rewards of completely satisfying his desires for food and the results of such action. Whether you give yourself excess, moderate or less than moderate fulfillment, you are a winner but you are also a loser. So it is totally up to you what you would rather win, what you want to lose, and what is most important to win and less important to lose.

But in your winning and losing, be advised that a person's winning is seen both in what he can do and in what he can prevent himself from doing. Power or strength is seen both in what you can do and what you can refrain from doing. A perpetually successful person is one who at times, and to certain things, wins, and at times to certain things, prevents himself from winning as it may appear to the opposite sect. A perpetually successful person is one who is a pro at educating his mind regarding what needs to be won and what needs to be lost in relation to his specific mission, regardless of what anyone else is trying to win. Ultimately, he must be able and willing to lose the benefits (whether physical, mental or emotional) which are outside of the direction of his travel or mission in order to gracefully win the satisfaction of striking his gold (goal). He must also be able and willing to prevent himself from taking baits that present themselves to delay and pull him in a direction outside of his intended travel or mission. They will most certainly delay or prevent him from striking his real gold. The reality is that you may win in your greed, but ultimately you will have lost.

Exile can be golden. There is still another kind of obstacle. These are called social obstacles. In this case, you are surrounded by friends who are very dear to you. They can sometimes be obstacles. They visit you so often that their demands on your time and resources infringe upon the time and resources that you need to invest into your cause. Your so-called friends, who demand of you the substance that is required to invest into your cause, are obstacles to your cherished dream. The resources that you need to accomplish your task are the very resources that your so-called friends demand from you.

Protect your resources... use them to enhance *your* dream or watch them dwindle away into enhancing someone else's dream. Your first responsibility is to develop *your* dream. In a secondary setting you may extend it to your 'neighbor.' To develop your dream is *your* responsibility. To reach out to your neighbor is a *favor*. In this case, your friends are obstacles of your cause. There is no doubt about it, you definitely need to do something about it. In this case, great tact is demanded. You might not be able to separate your obstacles from yourself easily, but if you can, without hurting them unnecessarily, you should. If the previous alternative is impossible, you must separate yourself from these obstacles. It may sound harsh but, as your friends are the obstacles in this instance, you must structure your resources to fully enhance your cause if you are going to reach your goal. You must get rid off them or at least redeem back the resources that you need to achieve your goal. It might seem like I am advocating some harsh measures here, but it's a scene that you will have to perform when it appears. It may also come down to where it becomes a solo scene with you alone in the drama. If that is the price that you must pay to own (earn) your designed reward, then that you must pay.

Separating the obstacles from your cause is a very challenging move and demands some necessary factors to be executed. The first of these is increased determination. By this, the writer means both an increase in determination to stay victorious over your obstacles and the determination to shoot for your goal. The second ingredient is increased dedication to your cause. By this, the writer is referring to a dedication so severe, no attraction or distraction, regardless of what it is, should be able to detour you from your cause.

Whatever can sidetrack or distract you will be your source of defeat, the substitute for your cause, and the price that was used to buy out your dream.

The third and final ingredient, perhaps the most important, is an increase in relaxation or self-confidence. *The term self-confidence in this context simply means to be satisfied with whatever you are doing.*

You might be uncomfortable with what you are doing because an action you have taken has triggered intense fire from its target. However, in every instance, if an action is first, pleasing to God, in a secondary way, progressive, and third, in context with your designed mission, you have every reason to be confident or satisfied with it.

The absence of satisfaction with what one is doing is the absence of self-confidence. To overcome this with less trouble, you need the ability, which is one of the most important abilities in a successful person. It is *"the zero ability"* or the ability to forget. Many people lack this ability because they need to practice it. Many people have ended up in mental institutions because they needed to develop this ability.

There are many things in your life both that you have done and that have been done to you, that you cannot and will never be able to reverse. These potential mountains can become plagues, and most of

What goes on backstage of the arena of achieving a dream

all, obstacles to your cause and success throughout the rest of your life. To prevent this from happening, you need *"the zero ability,"* the ability to forget and focus on your goal or goals.

Mind your own business. To focus and refocus is a daily chore. In some instances, this chore is narrowed down to a minutely, sometimes secondly chore. This means that the matter is so pressing that it comes down to you making sure that you are focused or focusing on your mission each second, not just daily; to ensure that you stay on course.

Pursue your mission within your normal rhythm. If you proceed outside of your normal rhythm, you will be out of coordination. If you proceed outside of a based perspective (the perspective that you are not better than anyone but are just an average human being focused or committed to a cause), you are bound to go off course.

It is therefore necessary for you to ensure that every moment of your day or life be delivered from a based perspective. It is your duty to supervise and regulate yourself daily and bring yourself to an harmonious state in which you are in harmony first with God, secondly with your cause and thirdly, with other people as much as possible. It is that premise from which you should operate every moment of the day.

Be current. Finally, we will examine the obstacle of living in the past. Don't live in the past, live from, or as a result of it. Learn lessons from your past mistakes and successes, failures and victories. Make sure that you pass the test the first time around so that you don't have to repeat it. Enjoy the foundation and structures that you have constructed in your past. Accept the losses that you have incurred from it but don't live in it.

By living in the past, you are living an outdated lifestyle. Your thoughts and actions would have been in the measurements, standards, requirements and events of the past while your real being, expectations and demands would be existing in the present. When you live in the past, your lifestyle definitely needs to be updated. Let's strive to deprogram our focus from yester-dates, yester-events, yester-statuses, except to program them as history and lessons. Let us now reprogram our focus and activities to today's dates, events, causes and requirements. Whatever we have to do to update our perspectives, that we must do if we are going to make our dreams come true.

A real visionary; commissioned, committed and accomplishing person can consciously and artistically make himself remember like a video recorder. He can do this when he wants to, with what he wants to, as it is necessary, and, with similar effort, compartmentalize the things that he chooses not to keep there to the extent where they are not sitting on his agenda.

Two very important skills that you, as a perpetually successful person, have to learn to do are: *1.) win, forget and proceed; and 2.) lose, forget and proceed.* If a person does not have the ability to forget, he might as well forget success in anything or even life as a whole. Did you get the message? Read it again if you didn't. It is a message that you will want to remember all your life if you intend to get anywhere.

A woman was suddenly struck by the death of her husband. She went to a pastor for counseling. The pastor said that, for once in his counseling ministry, he struggled to come up with an appropriate solution for that woman which could calm her spirit, comfort her and make her believe that life was still worth living.

What goes on backstage of the arena of achieving a dream

The reason was because he knew that what she was going through was real, personal, lasting and very present, he said. After searching long and hard, a thought finally dawned on him. He wasn't quite sure that it would work but it was the closest that his mind could come to something that might actually touch that woman. Per the pastor, he confessed to that lady that he had fallen short of an appropriate answer but, if it would help, the only answer he could give was this: *"start over again."*

I did not hear the result of his confession, but I can see that woman's face light up with delight as her heart took a 180 degree turn... a leap from hopelessness to hope; from desolation to restoration; from degradation to recreation, realizing that her best bet rested in this profound statement: *start over again!*

When people give you the shock of your life and you are shocked right out of your trust in them... your best bet is to start over again. When you have tried your best, and everything has gone up in smoke, your best bet is to start over again. When you get fed up of trying and your effort yields no satisfaction, don't give up, just start over again. When suicide becomes your only way out, please don't go all the way out, enter again with a completely new and better approach - start over again. And when you don't know what else to do and surrender is the only thing that's due, please go an extra mile. Don't accept that which is before you, start over again.

This time, give it everything you have and hunt through your life for all the extra resources you can muster up and throw them in with God as your master designer. The rest could be history, **rather, His story.**

CHAPTER 14

"Treasurize" Your Travel

Every person's "achieve-ability" depends greatly on his ability to prevent himself from being distracted and sidetracked.

Where is your treasure? One night, while working as a security guard at Bluebeard's Castle Hotel in St. Thomas, United States Virgin Islands, the many dilemmas of the nine-to-five syndrome was driven home to me by one of the people I had to work with. During that period, I was searching for the pieces of this book. It was a way to accomplish my dreams and escape from the shackle of the nine-to-five lifestyle. Suddenly, a golden idea hit me so hard, I haven't yet been able to recover. It permanently replaced all my former formulas and media of achievement. The thought was this: *"Give your treasure to your travel and your travel to your treasure."*

I went to one of my co-workers and presented the thought to him and asked him to ponder it for a while before I explained it.

About five minutes later I went back to him and asked if he fathomed the depth of the thought. He said, "Not quite." Well here was my golden opportunity to drop it like a bomb.

I proceeded by asking him if he ever heard of the statement *"where your treasure is, there your heart is"*. He said that he had.

I said, "Do you believe it?" He said, "yes." I said, "So wherever you invest, bank or store your treasure, there your heart will be, right?" He agreed.

"When your heart is involved in something, isn't that the highest state of involvement there is?" I asked. Again, he agreed.

So I said, since your heart is where your treasure is, if you want to get your heart to be involved in something, isn't it logical that you store your treasure in that direction or entity? Isn't that the formula to be wholeheartedly involved in something? If you wholeheartedly want to go in a certain direction isn't it logical that you invest, bank or store your treasure in that direction?

He said, "I got the part of giving your treasure to your travel, but I don't quite understand the part of giving your travel to your treasure."

After rethinking it, I realized that I couldn't completely blame him for not understanding "give your travel to your treasure." I should have said to him *"Give your treasure to your travel and you will automatically travel to your treasure."*

You might now be asking what I am really saying. I am glad you asked. Here is your part. Whatever you want to become or are striving for, give the thing that you treasure most to it and it will become the thing that you treasure most. Whatever your dream, give your best to it and it will reach out to you with its best. Give your best to your quest and you will reach your quest with great zest. Give all that you have, to what you want and what you want will become what you have. With your treasure already at or in the direction of where you want to go, do you think that's ample motivation to travel in that direction? A person's total treasure is himself first and his assets second. Do you get the point? To wholeheartedly travel to your "gold" you will first have to devote your entire self to it and second, devote all your assets to it. Each of us is given, by our Creator, the ability to develop the resources that are required to carry out our mission on this planet. At times, we find ourselves with less than is required to carry out our missions because of our poor budgeting skills throughout our lifetime. We have been given, by our Creator, enough inner and external resources to accomplish his plan for our lives, but we have often over spent those resources along life's path.

Progressive devotion is taking a dive from the head to the heart. To be wholeheartedly devoted to your cause is of paramount importance to the construction of your vocational empire as it is to the operation, duration and strength of it. The absence of devotion to one's cause is credited with failure to get into office and failure in office. A lack of devotion to one's cause results in failure to reach the top and failure at the top. A lack of devotion to one's cause is responsible for slow and no growth. A lack of devotion to one's cause is passive, vocational murder. A lack of devotion to one's cause is silent, "destinational" suicide.

You say, "how do I start to devote myself or what do I start to devote first and following to my cause?"

The first resource that you should devote to your cause is your mind. This requires a perpetual state of alertness and planning to make sure that your projects are diagramed properly and completed. This state is when you do not allow the intensity and importance of your cause to decrease or diminish but always to increase and remain alive. This state is when you dare to live your commitment instead of just declaring it. It is when you resolve to continue to stand firmly, instead of bowing to your obstacles; to stand straight, instead of bending to your attractions; to die doing it right, instead of living while doing it wrongly. This is when you resolve that, if required, you will become popular slowly and carry the right qualities with you up the ladder instead of becoming popular speedily and carrying nothing valid on your way there. This includes a constant rejection of the invalid, corrupted and self-centered ways and thoughts that will in the short or long run, always produce substance of their kinds.

The second resource that you must devote to your cause is your time. Time will always be transformed, either into past or progress. If it is transformed into progress, it did not just pass for you. If you did not transform it into progress, it is automatically transformed into the past... with nothing to show for it. It cannot be both; it becomes either one or the other.

Life is a mission of transforming time. It is a journey of networking with people in the realm of time. Time must be highly

What goes on backstage of the arena of achieving a dream

respected. It was here from the beginning of creation, and it will be here throughout our lifetime on earth. It is a worthy force to reckon with for as long as we live. Dr. Martin Luther King Jr., said that *"time is neutral."* It is we who have to transform it into production or progress.

Time is hours issued or distributed to everyone, including you and me. Your time needs to be properly scheduled into minutes and hours, days and dates and used with wisdom and accuracy.

It will make a big difference when you realize that twenty-four hours of the day belong to you, just as they do to the president or leader of your country. It will make a great difference when you realize that your success depends on how wisely or effectively you utilize these hours. Some people use them for folly. But the most important question to be answered in relation to your journey to your dream is not so much what will you use those hours for, but how many of them will you devote to your cause or mission.

Preserve your sleeping hours. Sleep like you're going away instead of like you are planning to stay stagnant. Remember that you have a future empire that you are working on in the present. I remember when I was a little boy living with my grandmother in the country. On some weekends I had to go to my mother who lived in town. I'd be up virtually all night before the morning when I had to get up early to catch the one bus to go to my mother.

When everyone else was fast asleep, I would doze off a little but my anxiety would wake me up much earlier than necessary. I would hear every rooster crowing that night and enjoyed every bit of it. My anxiety prevented me from going back to sleep for fear I would sleep beyond the time to get up and get dressed to catch the one bus that would pass through our district. Since I didn't have access to an alarm clock as most of us have today, those roosters crowing was my signal and I wasn't about to miss it. As a result, I welcomed their crowing. Though disturbing it may have been to others, it was music to my ear. I slept like I was going away that night and not like I was staying there, where I was at that time. Today, you have alarm clocks available to you, use them limitlessly!

There is no question about your necessary sleeping hours; the question is about the unnecessary ones. In most cases, you will not be able to get luxurious sleep if you are going to accomplish your task, but remember that it is unnecessary. It is actually a painful process to cut your luxurious sleep at first but with constant practice, it will become natural and a routine. You must practice until you become a pro at sleeping like you are going away instead of like you are here to stay. In case you need a reminder, remember that you are the agent of a future empire - yours. Also remember that you never have the future to build the future but rather, the present, this present. You will never have this present again.

You may be blessed with another present. This one is a one-time passer; it will never pass your way again. You might have another present to do something else but you have this to do this particular project. Therefore, don't rob yourself of your fulfilling sleep, but know yourself. Know how much sleep your body needs in order to perform and give yourself that amount of sleep without disturbance.

What goes on backstage of the arena of achieving a dream

No more or less is necessary. Some people can function on six hours of sleep each day, some on four. Others need eight or even nine. How many do you need? That you must know.

Preserve your leisure hours. Leisure hours are a privilege you must enjoy while they last. These hours are those spent with friends and other people, doing the things that you all enjoy, that do not necessarily involve or concern your cause. During these hours, you can forget your cause, tentatively let down your hair and have yourself a sobering picnic.

These hours are not wasted hours, if properly minimized or utilized. There is a difference between hours spent marking time and leisure hours. Hours spent marking time are hours spent burning up energy trying to reach a goal, and remaining stagnant. Remember that you are not in the military in this case. Nobody ordered you to mark time on their hours. You are on your own hours; in this case spend them moving. Leisure hours should be utilized only after your scheduled cause hours are properly spent and the scheduled work to be done within them is completed.

Wasted hours are earned hours "uninvested" or thrown in the garbage bin. Wasted hours are never wisely spent, never. Wasted hours are excessive or unnecessary hours spent on any area, any task, anything. It is so important that you catch this: *leisure hours are different from wasted hours. Wasted hours are going to be needed somewhere along the way.* These are the hours you stole from your cause that will prove missing somewhere in the budget or economy of your life or journey. The sad reality is that you will never be able to retrieve those wasted hours and contribute them to your cause or any cause. They are gone for good, though missing from the economy of the resources of your dream.

Charity hours are never wasted hours. The best investment after that, which is placed in God, is that which goes into people, including yourself. Charity hours are spent doing things for people outside of your job requirements. Hours spent on people are never wasted unless they are done in excess. Hours spent on other people are able investments for your unable returns. When you spend hours on other people you are investing in your sickbed treatment, your relatives' sickbed treatment and most importantly (the time when you can do nothing at all), you and your relatives' deathbed treatment.

Your cause hours are the center posts of empire building. The three forms of time for a visionary are: 1.) present; 2.) production and 3.) past. Which will you make it? The most important hours for a visionary are *his "cause hours."* The cause hours are the hours spent exclusively toward your cause or the advancement of your projects. These hours are the central hours of your success. Be warned that the other hours are to be utilized after your cause hours are properly and productively taken care of. They are not in the least to be minimized or substituted. Cause hours should be ringing in your ears, your mind and every motivating particle always, to the point of action, repeated action, continuous action and completed action. You do not necessarily have to plan any of the other hours ahead, but it is a must that you plan your cause hours. They must be properly planned and carried out with great determination and

What goes on backstage of the arena of achieving a dream

precision.

The next critical type of resource that you are to devote to your cause is *your physical labor*. This portion of your devotion can be another painful process at first. However, the more you sacrifice, the less painful it becomes. It will also become more of a routine. Regardless of how painful this process is at first, it is a must to be devoted to your cause if you are going to get anything done or reach anywhere. The more physical exercise you can afford, the easier it becomes.

This portion of your devotion is like the bridge of your success in anything. It takes you from planning to production and progress. Failure to apply this portion to your journey or the making of your dream, keeps you on the entrance side of your success instead of the exit side.

The next type of resource that you should devote to your cause is *your heart*. This is the highest level of resource available to you. Give this and you'll bid the rest good-bye. To reach this state of devotion is to be so devoted to your cause that you are no more a slave to it but are motivated by love for it. When you reach this stage, you will not seek merely to receive from your cause, but to give to it. This stage is when you give up all other causes that will in any way jeopardize this one cause and yield yourself to it totally.

This stage could very accurately be called the consummation stage. It is the stage when instead of you consuming the resources of your cause to extinction; your cause consumes you to the point of ultimate exclusivity. Every part of your being is given to this one cause. You are caught-up in total consummation with your course or your cause. This is the stage when you eat your cause, drink your cause, sleep your cause, wake your cause, talk your cause, walk your cause, play your cause, read your cause, write your cause; you name it. It is in everything that you do, say and think.

Give it your all and it will become your all. The final area of resource that you are to devote to your cause is your assets. To wholeheartedly travel to your gold, you will have to devote all your assets to it. You say, *"You can't be serious. Do you mean that I must devote my whole bank account, my whole family, my car and all that I own?"* Bingo! Only you've left out a few things that you didn't realize you had and might be forced to find and throw them in somewhere down the line.

Devoting any particular thing to something does not necessarily mean that you have to use up all of its contents at any one particular time, or on any one particular aspect of the journey. It does mean that it must be available for its use at anytime (in its totality if necessary) that its owner requires its use towards its survival and/or advancement.

One of the unavoidable factors that you will most certainly need to devote your assets to building, in traveling to your goal, is a large and comprehensive library. You should diligently seek to build both a mental and a geographical or now, digital library. The importance of this investment cannot be stressed enough. With this move, you will constantly learn trends in your field and how to properly operate in it.

CHAPTER 15
Your Success Quotes

1. Life is a journey of dreams coming true through you: yours or someone else's, which will it be?
2. The person who does not have a system for success automatically has a system for failure.
3. Sometimes you have to go into exile from the city of vultures - those who underestimate you, actively discourage or degrade you, are waiting for or calculating your failure before you fail; until your baby is born. This is like John on the Isle of Patmos until the book of Revelation was born [Rev. 1:9-20]; Moses in the backside of the desert 40 years until God was ready to present him to the public [Exodus 3]; Hannah in her moment of silence with God in her period of sorrow until she found favor in the eyes of the Lord [1 Samuel 1:13-18]; the apostle Paul in the desert of Arabia for three years in divine training until he was ready to

What goes on backstage of the arena of achieving a dream write 11 books of the NT and start numerous churches [Galatians 1:15-18]; Jesus in the garden of Gethsemane as He went "yonder" in one on one episodes with His Father in His period of deepest sorrow until He was ready to face the vicious Cross [Matthew 26:36-44].

4. Problems or disappointments will either prove something to you, in you, about you or all of them together.
5. Practice makes professionals and without practice, excellence is an impossibility.
6. The two basic motivational approaches are love and fear, to get and to get away from.
7. If it takes recalling four pages of your past victories to make you take one step forward, it will take recalling less than one page of your past failures to make you stay four steps behind.
8. Power is proven not by demonstrating what you can do only, but also what you can prevent yourself from doing.
9. A visionary is always professionally employed by, and diligently working for, his future and the future of his fellow human Brethren.
10. The best medium for making a famous person or organization is people (God initiated it).
11. The shortest distance between two points is a straight line and the shortest distance between your status and your intended status is a straight path.
12. The gold mine of every person's success is people and the gold is their support.

13. It is easier to get a person to bow to you by bowing to him first than by demanding that he bows to you first.
14. Watch the poison mouth; it can utterly wipe you out.
15. The secret of knowing a person is talking to him unlimitedly, while on guard, off guard, on an average day, in a pressuring situation; just talk to that person and take note of the responses.
16. The "excellency" of a person's "achieve-ability" depends greatly upon his ability to prevent himself from being distracted and sidetracked.
17. If your gold is in the west, you are off course if you are traveling northwest.
18. Initiate and instigate revolution in the right direction —people are easier led into doing right, than driven.
19. If one lacks the ability to deliberately forget, he might as well forget success.
20. As you grow in years, you will see that your enemies hardly get to hurt you – your "friend-emies" do.
21. The greatest spy of all time is time itself. Time reveals a multitude of secrets.
22. The person who has no respect for his boundaries is destined to lose his banners.
23. Most people, most of the time, give themselves the benefit of the doubt instead of giving it to their victims.
24. Fools invest in financial institutions; wise people invest in people. Invest in people and invest in yourself.
25. Mankind's only two friends are himself and his benefits.

What goes on backstage of the arena of achieving a dream

26. When you lose everything and everyone and your assets become just you, look up to your Maker and remember that everything and everyone else is luxury. Luxury is exactly that; it's not a necessity.

27. Every time a person approaches you, he/she is asking for something. It might just be attention and if you can identify that thing and furnish it each time, you can have the world eating out of your hand in no time.

28. Man's number one effective enemy is his mind. Nothing else usually is unless his mind deems it so.

29. The person who wants to conquer the world must get his mind to believe that he can; whatever it tells the body to do, it obeys.

30. The head of man's destiny is God and the head of his body is his mind. If you want to get the body to do something for you, consult its head, the mind.

31. The greatest ability of all is the ability to deliberately lose to definitely win.

32. The person, who has learned to successfully command himself to do the right before he is commanded to, has learned the true secret of freedom.

33. It is the ambition to perfect skills that makes experts, not the initial learning of them.

34. The hardest person to regulate is "me." My hardest task in life is to learn to regulate myself. I firmly believe that if I truly learned how to do that, I will have truly learned how to regulate others.

35. A plan is a private diagram; without it, you haven't started as yet, tiger!
36. Master the art of mastering yourself first, then you will have earned the right to master the art of mastering others.
37. It's a royal art to be silent enough to discern what people are really saying. What they say is not usually what they are saying. What they are saying is usually between what they say and how they say it.
38. There is more truth in what is not said than what is said.
39. The best way to kill a tree is to kill its roots. The best way to kill your support is to kill your supporters.
40. Bees are attracted to flowers because of their pollen, not their beauty. You will not win the world over by how tall you stand or how good you look, but only by what you can offer.
41. Quantity is numerable but quality is valuable.
42. If you don't pass the test before the contest, you won't pass it at the contest.
43. It is better to die on your way to a dream than to live for one day without one.
44. The walk of a mile is the total sum of steps.
45. Imitators cherish history; inventors make and shape it.
46. What is not said is a louder and more accurate language than what is said.
47. Many of the history makers weren't perfect or even near to it. They just amounted to an average person who was determined to achieve above average.

What goes on backstage of the arena of achieving a dream

48. People are quick to condemn, slow to compliment and slow to admit.
49. Take the camera off yourself and focus it on others for the rest of your life and see the world flock to you for their portraits.
50. The mind that harbors litter is a homebound garbage bin.
51. The moment that you stopped winning, you were a winner.
52. The average person who is unable to span or suppress you will declare that you are fat instead of big.
53. If you appear inferior, you are nice; if you appear equal, watch out; if you appear superior, hold up your gloves.
54. The "me" person seeks to address the defects in others and the perfection in himself. The "people" person seeks to address the good qualities in others while working on the defects in himself.
55. Every choice gives immediate or long-term gratification but carries an equivalent portion of short- or long-term consequence.
56. The bridges you burn today might be the ones you'll need to walk on tomorrow.
57. Your greeting can win you a place with its recipient or gain you a place with its recipient.
58. It is the appropriate or effective use of knowledge that is power, not knowledge alone.
59. The most apparently macho male or the most seemingly independent female that you can find anywhere can do very well with a dose or two of praise.
60. Remove human support from any person and extinction is his destination.

61. Truth has a way of staying alive under piles and piles of rubbish and, forgotten moons later, bursting through and growing as fresh and genuine as it always was.
62. The human being has two extreme mirrors: 1.) when he is given the upper hand and 2.) when he is in a state of struggle or his back is against the wall.
63. Make your investment so wisely that you'll smile all the way to eternity instead of to the bank.
64. When you engage God in making your calls for you, get off the line, hang up, put down the phone, keep your mouth shut and go take care of God's business. Leave yours to Him and let Him take care of it.
65. Television is one of the biggest "officialized" and most subtle killers of dreams.
66. "As the fining pot for silver, and the furnace for gold; so is a man to his praise." [Proverbs 27:21]
67. Humility is the resolve that though you have the right to excel within your own rights, it is within your own rights that you have the right to excel and the same right is given to everyone.
68. After you have done all that you can, you would have done all that you can. When you have done all that you can, then that's all that you can do. Leave the rest to God!